judith phillips, mo ray and
mary marshall

social work with
older people

fourth edition

palgrave
macmillan

D0234436

First edition (*Social Work with Old People*) 1983
Second edition 1990
Third edition (*Social Work with Older People*) 1996
Fourth edition 2006

Published by
PALGRAVE MACMILLAN
Houndmills, Basingstoke, Hampshire RG21 6XS and
175 Fifth Avenue, New York, N.Y. 10010
Companies and representatives throughout the world

PALGRAVE MACMILLAN is the global academic imprint of the Palgrave
Macmillan division of St. Martin's Press, LLC and of Palgrave Macmillan Ltd.
Macmillan® is a registered trademark in the United States, United Kingdom
and other countries. Palgrave is a registered trademark in the European
Union and other countries.

ISBN-13: 978–1–4039–1613–6 paperback
ISBN-10: 1–4039–1613–6 paperback

This book is printed on paper suitable for recycling and made from fully
managed and sustained forest sources. Logging, pulping and manufacturing
processes are expected to conform to the environmental regulations of the
country of origin.

A catalogue record for this book is available from the British Library.

A catalog record for this book is available from the Library of Congress.

10   9   8   7   6   5   4   3
15   14   13   12   11   10   09   08   07

Printed in China

Contents

List of illustrations

Figures

Table

Acknowledgements

We acknowledge those who taught us and inspired us to pursue a career in social work.

Mo Ray would like to acknowledge two older men, Hossain 'Ben' Khalif and Malcolm Johnson. Judith Phillips wishes to express her thanks to former colleagues – Sue Kirby, Dawn Penman, Pauline Carbury, Sue Perkins and Loraine Stewart. Mary Marshall wants to thank Judith Phillips and Mo Ray for undertaking the work on this book.

part

I

The social work context

Introduction

This book aims to inspire and inform social workers and social work students who want to know more about working with older people and their families. It will also be helpful for professionals who work with social workers and want to understand more about their special contribution. It is written by people with long experience in the field: in practice, as social workers, undertaking research in this field and teaching gerontology and social work. It is an introductory text with good grounding in some of the complex issues surrounding social work with older people and the assumption is that enthusiasts will move on to read what is now a very substantial literature about older people, if not about social work specifically. It is quite impossible for one book to cover the whole field thoroughly, but a book like this can whet the appetite and can point the direction towards further reading. Most of the relevant literature is not written specifically for social workers, and this book is a rich source of references to a very wide range of material.

Working with older people has many dimensions and raises many dilemmas. This book addresses a lot of topics and maps out many of the debates. We have aimed to target a beginning practitioner who has a special interest in older people. Social work with older people is complex and this book attempts to examine the values, skills and knowledge required to work with older people. In this way it provides a specific contribution to the literature. The past 15 years have seen a burgeoning of literature on old age and ageing, in addition to general texts on social work, which include chapters on working with older people. Many of these books have focused on community care and the developments in practice. However, few books in this period have attempted to bring together the frameworks for understanding social work with older people, for example, new areas of research and knowledge in gerontology while addressing the challenges in working as a social worker within and across organisations. In this sense, the book brings together gerontology with social work and synthesises the evidence base required to carry out the social work task.

Social workers who choose this field cannot be shrinking violets. Older people are not well served by social workers who do not question attitudes, resources and priorities. Ageism is rife and one manifestation is the widespread assumption that older people have simple needs such as for food, warmth, cleanliness and safety whereas the reality is that older people need effective and skilful practice. Simply filling in forms and brokering care are rarely an adequate response. The much overworked, and insufficiently practised, concept of community care can too easily become community neglect, at least of the unique individuality of each older person and their particular circumstances.

Social workers also need to be confident that they have something special to offer. Government policy is rightly pushing towards team-work and sharing skills, but this cannot be achieved to best effect unless everyone in the team knows what particular contribution they can make. There are large areas of overlap, but there are also very specific areas of knowledge and skill. We provide a clear picture of what we believe these to be. We also give very clear messages about a value base that emphasises participation, sharing information, being open about what we are doing and avoiding oppressive practice.

This is the fourth edition of this book. The first was published in 1983 in a very different world. The baby boom of the turn of the century was ageing and few social workers were interested. The field of gerontology was emerging. The pluralist economy of care was unknown.

Twenty years later, the shape of the ageing population is very different and we have experienced a great shift in the way services are delivered. We are also a lot wiser, both about social work with older people and of older people generally; there is now a very substantial body of research and writing. We can, for example, talk about the evidence base for some of our work although there a great deal more research is still needed. Similarly, a critical approach is being taken to issues surrounding ageing and social work, where established norms in relation to gender and care, for example, are being challenged.

The book is divided into two parts. Part I addresses the context of social work with older people and draws heavily on gerontological literature; Part II addresses practice issues. Throughout, we attempt to integrate both social work and gerontological literatures and provide a critical perspective that challenges traditional assumptions about older people. Chapter 1 maps out the crucial issues facing older people in our society today; how older people are defined, the situations in which they live, and what role they play in society. These aspects highlight the diversity of older people and highlight the context of ageing in Britain. Chapter 2 focuses on a case for social work, and asks who and under what circumstances does social work operate? Not all older people, even those in later life and in difficult circumstances will come the way of social work. The reasons for intervention are often the many and complex problems older people face. The chapter concludes by reviewing the guiding frameworks for intervention – theory, reflexivity, evidence or knowledge-based research, policy and legislation. Policy and its organisational context are discussed further in Chapter 3 which briefly looks at the historical development of services for older people and the changing nature of policy and legislation in the past 20 years. Despite the expansion of legislation and guidance and the introduction of the modernisation agenda, social workers face continued organisational constraints and pressures. This chapter addresses the difficulties of working in different social work contexts.

The role, tasks and skills necessary in social work are discussed in Part II. We follow a traditional approach in looking first of all in Chapter 4 at the practice skills required, and then at the stages in care management from assessment, through care planning, and monitoring to intervention. In conclusion, we look at future issues for the new social worker, enabling them to support and develop their professional practice. By reading this book we hope social workers will become critical practitioners reflecting on their practice and able to intervene more effectively in anti-oppressive, participatory and empowering ways.

Most people learn through stories and this book provides several. They come from real practice and are presented to enable the reader to think through the issues. As in all fields, and perhaps especially so for a low status group of service users, we need social workers who can reflect on their practice.

Throughout the book we draw on two types of case material, drawn from our experiences as social work practitioners and teachers to illustrate various points. First, one case study, Mrs Terrell, is discussed in several chapters of the book as an evolving situation and examines major areas of practice in complex and dynamic situations. Second, 'one-off' snapshots of practice appear in the text to illustrate or highlight a point throughout the book. It is hoped that they will encourage readers to reflect on the issues raised and to consider them with respect to their own practice. The longer case studies can be a useful tool for discussion and debate in a learning environment.

There are a number of terms which the reader will find repeated throughout the book. They reflect the critical perspectives from which we write and are defined below. We place the emphasis in the book on 'ageing' rather than 'old age'. This latter term, as we discuss in Chapter 1, is socially constructed and we prefer to take a longer lifecourse approach. Some may argue that ageing begins as soon as we are born! We also prefer to use the term 'older people' rather than 'the elderly', which stigmatises and homogenises the 50 years of life which can be experienced under this term. A great deal has been written about the 'third' and 'fourth' ages or the 'young' old (up to 75 years of age) and 'old' old in the literature. We move away from these false distinctions as ageing becomes an experience which we all share. Taking older people as people first and also as citizens reflects the value position which we adopt in this book. It is a position which has underpinned our professional work as practitioners, lecturers and researchers in the field of ageing.

We wish to introduce readers to the concept of gerontological social work as a significant area of work with an increasing knowledge base. This is a common term used in the United States to distinguish this as an area of practice with a history and established evidence base. It is our hope that this book will mark the beginning of a trend in gerontological social work in the UK, which not only has applicability here but worldwide as other societies grapple with similar issues surrounding an ageing population.

Two points need to be made in this Introduction. The first point is that this book refers to English legislation and UK government policies and documents alone. Most of these apply to Wales too. The first three editions covered all the nations of the UK but this has become increasingly difficult as the four nations develop in their own way. There is a huge plethora of legislation and documentation which would drown the text. Readers in Scotland, Northern Ireland and Wales, however, will still find this book entirely relevant. There are far more similarities than differences (except perhaps free personal care). All nations have policies on social care, closer co-operation between health and social work, attending to the needs of carers, user consultation and greater monitoring of standards.

The second point is that the writing of this book was not shared equally. The book was almost entirely written by Judith Phillips and Mo Ray. Mary Marshall simply provided some comments. Mary Dixon who wrote most of the third edition provided a case study. Mary Marshall's name remains on the book to provide some continuity and to emphasise that social work with older people has a history not a great deal longer than this book.

This book can be read from beginning to end but can also be 'dipped into'. It provides further references to texts which cover issues in greater depth and several websites are also referenced which will help readers keep up to date with the issues. At the end of each chapter is a section called 'Putting it into practice', setting out two or three exercises which may be helpful in reflecting on the chapter. As you work through the book, you will develop your knowledge, understanding and skills in relation to social work with older people. Alongside this, you will develop a critical and reflexive perspective developing your analytical skills and your ability to use research in practice.

1 | Critical themes and issues in ageing

In this chapter we set the scene for the context of social work with older people by outlining the key themes and issues in ageing. We deliberately take a critical gerontological approach from the outset. This is in preference to presenting basic facts and figures and outlining the problems older people face. Although social workers will need to know details and consequences of population ageing, they also need to reframe some perspectives through which older people have been stereotyped, for example, as burdens on society by virtue of their numbers and being dependent on family members. Social workers will by the nature of their role and tasks deal with the most socially excluded older people with the most complex needs in society, but they need to take a wider perspective to look at the diversity of ageing and view experiences in later life in a positive light, rather than treating ageing necessarily as a negative experience. Even when people face crises, the strengths they have developed and demonstrated throughout their lifecourse need to be acknowledged. It is imperative that social workers understand and take a critical gerontological approach in their practice if they are to work effectively with older people in an anti-discriminatory way.

It is important, first, to look at the people we are talking about and the situations faced by an ageing population. After defining and critically evaluating the concepts of 'ageing' and 'old age', we look at the diversity of the older population in terms of structural factors such as gender, ethnicity and class. We then move on to look at the differences in how people experience ageing and later life based on differences in location, housing and living arrangements and health. All these factors, along with more individual factors, such as social relationships and social support (particularly from carers) will have an impact on their quality of life. The challenge for social work is to operate within this diverse context in a positive way and to challenge the myth that ageing is inevitably a period of decline.

Defining ageing: what is 'old'?

There have been shifting definitions of 'old' throughout history. Whereas two hundred years ago someone aged 40 seemed 'old', today they would be considered 'young'. Legal institutions and bureaucracies have notions of 'old', for example, retirement ages at 60 and 65 in the UK, free bus passes available at 60 or the requirement to renew a driving licence at 70. Definitions and expressions of age also differ across cultures, for example, in Bosnia, old age is not linked to chronological age or external appearance but a 'loss of power' (Vincent, 2003, p. 15) referring to both physical and social strength.

Longevity has been the success story of modern society with more of the population living longer into old age. The number of centagenarians in Britain continues to rise (Dalley and Smith, 1997). The definition of 'old' has stretched beyond imagination. At the turn of the century, a boy born in 1901 could expect to live to 45 and a girl to 49; today those figures are 75 and 80 years respectively (Office of National Statistics, 2003). General improvements in public health, housing, better food supplies and better working conditions have greatly improved our standard of living. This has meant more people have survived beyond infancy and lived into adulthood. The 2001 census data show that the ageing of the UK population is particularly evident when the number of people aged over 85 is considered. On census day 1951, there were 0.2 million people aged 85 and over (0.4 per cent of the total population). By census day 2001, this had grown to just over 1.1 million (1.9 per cent of the total population) (ONS, 2003). Predictions for 2031 suggest a rapid rise in the population over the age of 85 and over, which will then comprise 3.8 per cent of the UK population (www.statistics.gov.uk 2004). It is the rapid increase in the proportion of the 85-plus age group in comparison to older people in general that is significant for the planning of social and health care services, as disability tends to increase with later life. Whether as a society we will be able to sustain such increases in longevity is a moot point as obesity in childhood, inadequate diet and lack of exercise with increases in alcohol consumption threaten this trend.

Our subjective assessment of age is, however, governed by other definitions of age – imposed through the age of retirement (60 for women and 65 for men in the UK) or through health rationing (for example, until recently, breast cancer screening was offered on the NHS to women aged between 50 and 65 only, suggesting that older people over this age did not suffer from breast cancer. It has now been extended to age 70 (Kings Fund, 2002). Similarly, health and lifestyle advice is not always offered to older people although many older people are unaware that their lifestyles are unhealthy (Age Concern, 2000). The definition of 'old' is therefore flexible and a construction of society. For example, as a response to a pensions crisis in 2003, the UK government equalised retirement ages between women and men and proposed later life working beyond the 2003 formal retirement age. A further construction of age is the difference between the 'young' old, generally considered between 60 and 75 and the 'old' old over 75. This distinction continues to be arbitrary but is a powerful one in the discussion of the demographics of age. However, as differing lifestyles become a choice for any age, the distinction is increasingly blurred and an erroneous one to make. A more flexible approach is to consider the process of ageing rather than a fixed period of old age; in this sense we all share in the process (Thompson, 1995). This blurring of stages of the lifecourse has become a popular view of postmodernists (Featherstone and Hepworth, 1989) as discussed in Chapter 2. The 'mask of ageing' describes the experience where one's subjective age and external appearance are at odds with each other (Biggs, 1997). This has relevance for social work, particularly in assessing presenting needs.

What defines old age and its associated experiences will be dependent on factors other than chronological age. Bond, Coleman and Peace (1993), argue that age is less significant than class. Older people with high incomes and resources have more in common with younger people with similar incomes and resources than other older people without such resources; being a similar age does not mean a similar experience of ageing.

Lifestyle choice, rather than fixed stereotypes of age, has been increasingly a feature of 'active ageing' or 'positive ageing'. At one extreme, older people are seen as youthful and living 'designer lives' (Featherstone and Hepworth, 1989). This optimistic view of old age has been pursued by business as older people provide new marketing opportunities as consumers with money to spend.

Ageing for the two sets of 'baby boomers', for example, those born between 1946 and 1950 and 1961 and 1965 will be a different experience from those people born earlier in the twentieth century. The first cohort of 'baby boomers', although born in a period of post-war austerity, lived through the 'swinging sixties', rock and roll, Vietnam and 'flower power'. This is clearly a far cry from their parents' generation and earlier cohorts who lived through the Second World War, rationing, Glen Miller and big band music, and Lyon's corner houses. For the second cohort born into prosperity between 1961 and 1965, access to occupational pensions, home ownership and the potential to accrue capital through investments allowed greater potential consumer power; yet they also experienced the recession of the 1970s with many never experiencing a permanent full-time occupation and growing inequality (Evandrou, 1997). Differences in terms of life expectancy, savings, relationships, pension payments and rewards will be evident between these two cohorts (Evandrou, 1998). The second 'baby boomer' group are set to be the wealthiest cohorts of older people. The contrast may be even greater between generations growing up using modern technology, the Internet, email and international travel. The ageing experience, however, may be very different again for those ageing without access to such resources.

Similarly, as we discuss later in this chapter, social resources through family and friends are an important factor in later life and family life has changed with rising divorce rates, reconstituted families, later marriages and age-gapped families, along with geographical distance between generations. This also means that different generations and cohorts will experience family life very differently. Unlike any previous generation, a larger percentage of older people over the age of 60 will be entering old age as divorced; having experience of second or multiple marriages and partnerships and may have a large network of step-children and grandchildren. With remarriage and divorce, older people may experience a transition to other intimate partnerships discovering, perhaps for the first time, their sexual orientation. More liberal attitudes toward gay and lesbian relationships will be available to them in later life than at any other stage in their lifecourse.

Increasingly, healthy older people enjoy activities traditionally associated with 'youth' such as hiking, mountain climbing, biking and flying. These experiences are no longer exceptional. Older people contribute significantly in all areas of social life, for example, through ongoing provision of support (practical, emotional, financial) to adult offspring and significantly, to grandchildren and to family members needing care. They also participate in a range of citizenship roles (for example, the magistracy, parish councils, prison monitoring boards, all of which, however, have age cut-off points) and through the provision of human resources, skill and expertise in the voluntary sector.

At the other extreme, there are older people who have experienced poverty for much or all of their lives. Being socially excluded, for example, from owning good quality housing, from regular paid work, from access to health care, and from living in vibrant communities, are often the associated consequences of living in poverty. In older age, people may be experiencing a continuity of poverty, which could be worsened by ageing (for example, as a result of widowhood or the experience of illness). Older people may have managed during their lives but, because they have no pension or financial resources, may experience poverty in retirement. The National Audit Office (2002) states that 2 million pensioners are classified as living in low-income households. This problem is exacerbated by the consistently low take-up of benefit entitlements (for example, pension credit, council tax relief and housing benefit). Scharf et al. (2002) reported that 45 per cent of older people living in three deprived areas in England could be defined as poor. That is, older people living in economically and socially deprived areas of England appear to be at least twice as likely to experience poverty as those in Britain as a whole.

It is essential that age and ageing are thought about as a heterogeneous experience and process, rather than assuming that 'the elderly' are a group of people who are very similar to, or the same, as each other. Underpinning heterogeneity are the critical issues of diversity of ageing and the lifecourse. The older population is as diverse as the population anywhere else in the lifecourse. Consideration of the gendered nature of ageing and the experience of people from minority ethnic groups illustrate this point.

Older women: the 'feminisation of ageing'

The world of 'old age' is a world of women. The only exception is among some black and minority ethnic groups where men over

60 clearly outnumber women (www.statistics.gov 2004). Women continue to live longer than men; boys and girls born in 2000 can expect to live to 75 and 80 years respectively (ONS, 2003). The difference in longevity is attributed to men being more likely to experience acute and life-threatening illness which may result in mortality whereas women are more likely to experience long-term, chronic and disabling conditions (Ginn and Arber, 1995). Increased longevity for women, together with features common to women's lives, results in particular consequences for older women. For example, traditionally, women have tended to marry men older than themselves and this means they may be more likely to care for their husbands, and are more likely to be widows. In 1995, 32 per cent of women aged between 65 and 74 were widows compared to 10 per cent of men of the same age range (OPCS, 1995) Chambers has commented that 'widowhood is the likely circumstance of older women and it becomes the norm as they move into old, old age' (2000, p. 127). It also follows that women experience widowhood for longer durations than their male counterparts. Without support from a male spouse, women who are widows, and become disabled and ill are more likely than men to enter residential care (Arber and Ginn, 1991). The same is true for women who have never married.

Women, particularly those in their eighties in 2004, are also more likely to have had sparse or interrupted work records. This is because married women in the 1930s, 1940s and 1950s were discouraged from working (apart from during the war) or if they did work, they were likely to have experienced significant disruptions for child care and family caregiving. Moreover, part-time and low paid work meant that women were paid less than their male counterparts and equal pay did not exist for much of the past century. Given the potential for interruptions to work, or a lack of paid work, women are much less likely to have contributed to their own pensions, or their pension contributions are inadequate (Arber and Ginn, 1995). This means that older women, especially those living alone, are more likely to be reliant on state pension provision and older women, living alone are likely to be the most deprived. Help the Aged (2003) state that only 49 per cent of women receive the full basic state pension, compared with 92 per cent of men. Acquiring a pension through a husband's earnings is becoming increasingly risky because of the propensity of divorce and collapse of the male breadwinner model (Crompton, 1999) with no guarantee of the husband accruing pension contributions. A gender-oriented pension policy which takes into account the caring commitments of women through their lifecourse is essential, if poverty is to be avoided in older age (Ginn, et al., 2001).

Although the social networks of older women are more extensive than men, the majority of older women whom social workers meet will be living alone. Some 50 per cent of women aged 75 and over live alone compared to 32 per cent of men of similar age (ONS, 2001a). Increasingly living alone is becoming a choice for older people, but for the majority of older people it is a situation they find themselves in after the loss of a partner, divorce and wider socio-economic circumstances. However, living alone may become a common experience for future cohorts of older people. Since the 1990s it has been an increasing trend for people under retirement age (Hall et al., 1999) and may remain so as this cohort ages. With living alone increasing for women in higher socio-economic groups with the benefits of independence being stressed, this will have consequences for future ageing populations in terms of community planning, housing and support.

In reviewing care services, social care is often viewed in gender-neutral terms. Until the 1980s women were invisible in social policy. However, this situation has changed and care services are increasingly gender-sensitive. In residential care, for example, women over the age of 85 are over-represented, along with those older people who have previously lived alone. Increasingly issues over the funding of long-term care, the closure of care homes and the movement of older people between care homes, when they can no longer afford to pay or where homes have closed, have had a disproportionately negative impact on women in residential care.

There is circularity in the feminisation of this caring relationship. Many of the people living in care homes are women, cared for by women who may be engaged in informal care (for relatives) as well as in a formal (paid) capacity (Cameron and Phillips, 2003). Work routines in care homes may facilitate part-time employment to enable women to manage other caring responsibilities, and the pay and conditions are often at the national minimum. The scene is set for future generations of women engaged in this type of work to experience the poverty of their older sisters.

Cuts in community services, particularly in relation to transport, are also likely to affect women significantly. Women are more likely to rely on public transport than men and generally have less opportunity to drive cars than men, thus, in later life, accessibility becomes a heightened issue, particularly for women living at some distance from services and family.

Older men have traditionally been discussed in the literature on ageing in their role as retirees from work (Phillipson, 1982), their dependence on services following bereavement (Arber and Ginn, 1991), and more recently, male identity (Courtenay, 2000) and their role in the spousal care relationship (Rose and Bruce, 1995; Davidson et al., 2000; Calasanti, 2003). In gerontology, however, the study of masculinity has traditionally been ignored (Calasanti, 2003) and the 'female script' has been taken as the predominant experience, partly because men were not seen as 'problems' and consequently have not been researched to the same extent as women. However, we are now realising that men do not fit the stereotypes portrayed through the female lens, for example, increasing proportions of men will live alone over the age of 65 (Davies et al., 1998) and fewer with a spouse which is the image portrayed of the 'old man'. Male caring is also becoming a common experience, particularly among spouses.

Ethnicity

The numbers and experiences of people from minority ethnic groups mirror differing patterns of migration to and within the UK. There are more than twice the numbers of people from minority ethnic groups in Britain now than in 1991, constituting 4 per cent of the older population (www.statistics.gov 2004; White, 2002). Too often the literature has grouped all ethnic minority groups together when talking about responding to an ageing Britain. Yet there are differences in ageing structures of various groups, resulting from the pattern of migration from countries of origin. Two-thirds of the black and ethnic population aged 60 and over are represented by black Caribbean and Indian communities and the remaining third are represented by black Africans, Chinese, Bangladeshis, Pakistanis and other groups (Qureshi, 1998; www.statistics.gov.uk 2004). Patterns of migration also point to different experiences for groups of black and minority ethnic people. The experience of ageing for people from black and minority ethnic groups must be underpinned by an awareness of diversity rather than assumptions about homogeneity. There is an increasing literature and research base on the experiences of older migrants in the UK, which overturns the previously held stereotypes of 'family looking after their own' (Atkin and Rollings, 1996; Butt et al., 2003), but there is increasing evidence that traditional services are geared up to a white population and institutional racism excludes people from black and minority ethnic groups from accessing services. Indeed, research evidence confirms that minority ethnic groups face the same issues as the majority white population, particularly in terms of the stresses of caregiving (Blakemore and Boneham, 1994; Atkin and Rollings, 1996; Phillipson et al., 2003). Many of these needs are met by black voluntary organisations that often face the uncertainties of short-term funding.

Other structural disadvantages and the effects of racism may compound these issues. Norman (1985a), in her hypothesis on triple jeopardy, highlighted the ways in which multiple experiences of exclusion and disadvantage, promoted by oppression and discrimination, deny people from minority ethnic groups full rights to citizenship. Phillipson et al. illustrate the experience of multiple disadvantages in their study of Bangladeshi women living in Tower Hamlets and comment: 'The depth of social exclusion illustrated by inadequate housing, poor health and low incomes underlines the case for an urgent, targeted response within social policy' (2003, p. 67). The implication for social work here is to recognise the social conditions and factors that constrain and exclude minority ethnic groups and to work with them in empowering ways to overcome disadvantage. Phillipson et al. also examined problematic caring relationships among Bangladeshi participants and argued that extended families, rather than reducing need, actually increased it. In this study, people reported suffering from language barriers, poor knowledge of resources and their difficulties were compounded by the running down of resources and services in deprived inner city areas. In this study, one woman, Mukta (with seven children) sums up her experience:

> The lifts don't work and there are always boys having drugs on the stairs. It is very frightening. The main door is supposed to be locked but they break it. They always break the lifts. Me

and my husband are both not well and it is difficult for him to climb all these stairs.

(2003, p. 32)

A study of older Chinese people by Chau and Yu (2000) concludes that social inclusion for participants was compromised by a number of barriers, such as language and lack of family support to help sustain intergenerational relationships. As well as identifying some practical developments to remove those barriers, the authors high-light the importance of starting where older Chinese people would wish to start and this inevitably means adopting clear and robust strategies for their meaningful participation and involvement.

Health

A further area of difference between older people is in relation to their health; such diversity will increasingly be significant for social workers to appreciate as health becomes a major area in assessment, and health professionals are key actors in multi-disciplinary work.

The majority of older people are healthy and live independent lives; consequently, old age should not be associated with disease. Even when people self-report their health, more than a third over the age of 75 say their health is good. Even living with a long-term health condition does not necessarily mean that older people would rate their subjective well-being negatively or indeed, their overall quality of life (Siddell, 1995).

However, health problems can affect larger numbers of people in later life. For example, the Living in Britain survey (ONS, 2001b) notes that 38 per cent of men and 28 per cent of women aged over 65 reported hearing impairments. Older women more than men report difficulties with their eyes – 31 per cent and 25 per cent, respectively. Older women are more likely than men to suffer chronic illness or functional disability (Arber and Ginn, 1991) and are more likely to rate their health as poorer. The impact of conditions such as arthritis on mobility is well known, and 23 per cent of the population aged 65 and over reported permanent mobility difficulties (ONS, 2001b). Overall, elderly women were more likely to report permanent mobility difficulties than men (27 per cent and 19 per cent respectively). The ONS Survey in 2001 also showed that the numbers of older people with permanent health difficulties increased with age with 11 per cent of people aged 65–69 reporting permanent difficulties compared with 60 per cent of people aged 85 and over. Living with such disabling conditions requires some adjustment to daily routine and activity.

Mental ill-health may also be an experience in older age; this may be because a person has had long-standing mental health needs and has aged with them, or because a person has developed mental ill-health in later life. While dementia can affect people through the whole lifecourse, its prevalence is higher with increased age. The Alzheimer's Society (2003) estimates that dementia currently affects over 750 000 older people in the UK. Over 18 000 people diagnosed with dementia are under 65. Data on diagnosis suggest that dementia affects 1 person in 20 aged 65 and over and 1 person in 5 aged 80 and over.

Based on prevalence and incidence statistics, the Alzheimer's Society estimates that by 2050, the number of people with dementia will have risen to over 1.5 million people. Clearly, it is essential that planning takes account of these changes and there will be a vital role for social workers in this context. The experience of dementia and the potential social work role in dementia care are discussed in Chapters 4 and 5 of this book.

Depression can affect anyone but it is more common in older people than any other age group. The Mental Health Foundation (2003) estimate that 10–15 per cent of older people living in the community show symptoms of depression but this figure rises to approximately 40 per cent when considering older people living in care homes. Depression may be caused by the experience or difficulties in managing or coping with bereavement, loss and change. People may also become depressed as a result of untreated illness; it is easy to imagine, for example, how unmanaged or untreated pain experienced over periods of time can result in a person feeling low and depressed. Many people have depression and dementia, with depression often going undiagnosed in these circumstances. Medication (for example, antibiotics, anti-parkinsonian, antipsychotic drugs) and its side effects can also be a cause of depression. This is an important consideration as 70 per cent of older people take prescribed medication on a regular or long-term basis (DoH, 2001a). At a practical level, this may be a major contributory factor in the high incidence of depression among older people living in care home environments as the population of older people living in care homes are more likely to be receiving medication for a range of illnesses and conditions. Moreover, the evidence is that older people are often over-medicated (Jackson, 1996: www.SocietyGuardian.co.uk); this may be particularly an issue for older people with dementia who are perceived as having 'challenging behaviour' and may be given medication to manage their behaviour (Jackson, 1996). The potential for age-based discrimination in the context of mental health is an issue which is of concern to older people affected, their families and practitioners (Age Concern, 2002).

Older adults, as with any group in the population, can also experience problems with alcohol (The Mental Health Foundation, 2003), and men are at significantly greater risk than older women, although this is changing. Alcohol abuse can be unrecognised among older people; this may be, to a significant extent, caused by ageist assumptions (for example, that older people do not drink alcohol in excess). This is likely to be a particular issue for people who develop problems with alcohol in later life, rather than people who have had a long-standing problem. Warnes and Crane (2000) highlight a strong relationship between homelessness and heavy drinking.

Class and income

In old age the effect of class and income is amplified through retirement. Class influences lifestyles in older age. Additionally, the lower the socio-economic status of an older person, the more likely it is that they will experience ill-health. Contributing to an occupational pension, owning property, accruing savings and retiring on a high income (Thompson, 1995) will also influence financial health in later life. In the past 30 years the increasing importance of a non-state pension has resulted in a growing inequality between those who have and those who do not have occupational pensions. Redundancy, unemployment, care for dependent children or adults all have a significant impact on the ability of people to accrue such pension (Falkingham, 1998; Gunnarsson, 2002; Evandrou and Glaser, 2003). Low public pensions are increasingly meaning a reliance on means-tested top-up benefits, with a quarter of all older people in Britain dependent on Pensioner Credit or entitled to it but not claiming it (Vincent, 2003). Inequality between generations is a current issue and the UK government attempted to address this issue with limits on welfare being concentrated on those most in need and an encouragement to private provision and saving for the majority of society. With the erosion of the state pension and increases in public expenditure and the council tax, older people are finding a political voice.

Location

The socio-economic and demographic factors discussed above divide the older population in a number of ways. These are also linked to where people live, as the experience of ageing will also be affected by diversity in where older people live, for example, between rural and urban environments; in cities, and in and between different countries. Although it is beyond the scope of this book to highlight global differences in ageing, placing Britain relative to other countries does throw some light on the relative position of older people in Britain today.

The majority of the world's population of older people (61 per cent) live in poorer countries, many where life expectancy remains below 50 (www.who.int/imp 2003). In 2004 globally about 1.2 billion people were living on an income of less than $1 per day and about 100 million of these are older than 60 (Petersen, 2004).

Trends in Britain reflect more general trends at a European level. Low fertility levels and extended longevity mean that the EU population is ageing, particularly those over age 80. At the same time the population of working age is dwindling; in 2001 the old age dependency ratio (the population aged 65 and over as a percentage of the working age population 15–64) had risen to 24.6 per cent; an increase of 4 per cent in 10 years (Eurostat, 2002). This continuing trend will have implications for social policy in all EU member states and, even with the more balanced demographics of the new accession states, this will remain a significant issue on the migration agenda.

Moving from a European level to a country level, significant differences in the experiences of ageing are found in urban and rural areas. For some older people there is a choice of migrating to warmer climates of other countries or to the seaside. This next section discusses such differences in location and the movement between areas. Social workers also need to understand the importance of 'place' to older people and the difficulties that distance can pose to older people, particularly if they are in need of care.

Older people living in rural areas may face a lack of services and difficulties accessing any limited provision. The experience of older people living in rural areas is influenced by factors such as poor transport, centralisation of services and resources, and poor service provision (Pugh, 2000). Older people living in rural communities may express need in terms of loneliness and isolation, accentuated by depopulation, the purchase of local houses as second homes and holiday houses, and the loss of personal networks through geographical mobility and bereavement. Pugh has argued that the increasing trend towards managerialist social work has meant that the wider social, emotional and psychological needs of older people are ignored in favour of the provision of practical services. This, of course, is not just an issue for older people living in rural environments. Clearly, there is a need for welfare and social care services to develop in the context of familiarity with the area and the population that it serves. While it may seem sensible to provide extra resources for a day centre in the main town to accommodate older people living in scattered villages 10 miles away, to the older people in question, travelling 10 miles to town for a few hours may feel unfamiliar, stressful and unnecessary.

Ageing in the inner city, however, does not necessarily mean that older people will have easy access to a range of support services. Many older people live in deprived inner city areas with poor resources. Scharf et al. (2002), in their study of ageing in three deprived inner city areas, highlighted that 34 per cent of respondents identified the lack of social clubs or community centres for older people in the neighbourhood. Other locations that superficially appear to be satisfactory may also not meet the needs of older people; urban regeneration, for example, can create environments suitable for professionally mobile couples but facilities that are important to other citizens have exited the area. Suburban areas too may suffer from poor transport links or out-of town shopping centres may cause the demise or deterioration of more traditional town centre shopping areas accessible to older people without public transport.

Location may also be an important factor encouraging movement in later life. For several decades, retirement migration has been a feature of British society. King et al. (2000, p. 5) identify five changes in twentieth-century society that have had a strong influence on aspirations of later life. They are:

1 The growth of retirement.
2 Increased survival rates (and therefore, longer retirement).
3 Greater affluence.
4 Improved education.
5 Better quality housing.

These factors have contributed to large numbers of people leaving urban and suburban settings for coastal and rural towns and villages. In some areas, for example, Worthing, the impact of retirement migration has significantly altered the demography of the population and impacted on service provision, particularly where social networks have not been established in the new area (Karn, 1977). Increasingly, wealthier older people are moving abroad to places such as Southern Spain and Italy to savour the benefits of the climate. However, this also poses a number of potential problems in respect of future welfare provision, which King et al. (2000) highlight as an issue that is yet to be faced in the context of European migration.

Location takes on increasing significance as generations live further apart from each other. This not only has implications for regular social contact and support but also for the quality of relationships and provision of care. With increasing globalisation and migration, issues of support to older people come into focus. Geographic proximity is the major element in solidarity between family members. Children who live long distances away from their parents experience considerable conflict and cope with anxiety and stress through telephone and email contact (Baldock, 2000). Connidis (2001) found that ambivalence in relationships could also be created through distance. Thus, proximity, distance and movement become particularly significant when care needs arise. Joseph and Hallman (1998) found that stress and interference with work resulted from the spatial arrangements of home, work and older relative. Having to travel in different directions to work and to the home of an older relative around work time can be stressful.

Long distances come into sharp focus for ethnic communities engaged in transnational caring (Phillipson et al., 2001). Schiller et al. (1992, p. 5) describe such people as 'transmigrants' who link their country of origin and their new country of settlement, sustaining familial, social and economic relationships and taking actions such as decision-making across boundaries. Sending money home for the care of older relatives linked several generations in Phillipson et al.'s (2001) study.

Housing and communities

In considering crucial issues in ageing, which have particular relevance for social work, housing is a key factor. Community care policies are underpinned by the principle of 'keeping people at home for as long as possible' and promoting independence rather than requiring a move to specialist provision when care needs arise. Housing has a crucial role to play in this equation as people 'age in place'. Housing conditions and housing tenure also play significant roles in the quality of life (Hughes, 1995). The Joseph Rowntree Foundation (2000) highlights the importance of good quality housing to health and well-being; however, it found in an analysis of community care plans that housing was often not discussed in the plan, even when they came from areas where housing was more likely to be sub-standard. There is great diversity in housing wealth, with 15 per cent of older homeowners being income and equity poor; 5 per cent being both income rich and equity rich. Further diversity in housing can be seen in relation to ethnicity, housing status and rural/urban location (Heywood et al., 2002). Older people are more likely to be living in sub-standard inappropriate housing stock, which lack basic amenities. The English Housing Conditions Survey (Office of the Deputy Prime Minister, 2003) indicates that 35 per cent of older people were living in an unsatisfactory home but were 'much more likely to do so where they are low income private sector households, the oldest person is 85 years old, or they have lived in their home for 30 years or more' (2001, p. 11). Older people are also twice as likely as younger people to live in rented accommodation. The Living in Britain survey (ONS, 2001b) indicated that 27 per cent of older people were tenants or joint tenants. Older people, particularly older women, may reside in private rented accommodation and be vulnerable to the commitment of landlords to maintain homes to a decent standard.

In the past, sheltered housing has been seen as a viable alternative. The initial intentions of sheltered provision to provide companionship and community life as well as enable independence, however, backfired with an increasing tendency to be dependent on the warden. Some schemes which were designed with one small bedroom in particular were also 'hard to let' (Tinker et al., 1995) and there was no evidence to suggest that sheltered housing led to a reduction in residential or nursing home care admissions. Such special needs housing for older people was seen as 'ageist' (Stewart et al., 1999) and rooted in focusing on the deficits of older people rather than the inadequacy of planners and architects. Similarly, 'Staying Put' and 'Care and Repair' schemes come under fire for the same criticism. However, this has led to an under-investment in both specialist and ordinary housing.

The debate has mainly been about whether housing should be a specialist provision for older people (segregation) or whether ordinary generalist housing is a better option (integration), yet in recent years age-segregated housing has taken on a new and different dynamic. Rather than be seen as a welfare provision, older people are buying into an identity of active lifestyle and participation through retirement communities. Although well established as a provision in the USA, it is only recently that this form of living arrangement has taken off in the UK with different models appearing (e.g. from the leisure village idea to the continuing care model). Research shows that there are a number of benefits to this way of living, such as an improved sense of health and well-being (Bernard et al., 2003). There has also been a widespread critique describing retirement communities in the USA in particular as geriatric ghettos, segregated from intergenerational community life where residents don't always agree on how the environment should be structured and where the retirement communities do not always embrace residents with disabilities. They have also been criticised for their leisure rather than their care orientation – they are more about helping people come to terms with retirement status than providing care to older people in later life (Metsch, 1996).

Separate from housing but of increasing significance is the work on 'the meaning of home'. The definition of 'home', however, has been regarded as a domestic setting with all its associated memories but less attention has been applied to this principle once older people have entered residential care. Although the principle is to make the residential facility as 'homely' as possible, when tested, a home for life is sometimes what it is not (e.g. Cowl and ORS v Plymouth

City Council, 2001). On the microlevel there are other issues that concern social workers, for example, there are issues regarding the extent to which older people with 'antisocial behaviour' (such as noisy or violent neighbours; or those living alone and at risk because of dementia) should remain in their own homes.

The significance of home is, however, taking precedence in housing policy to encourage initiatives for people to remain in their own homes. The use of technology will have a profound effect on our housing provision in this respect. There have been a number of initiatives in this arena which assist older people. Three are briefly outlined below:

1 Lifetime homes to meet the needs of all the family are of increasing significance, initially termed 'multi-generational housing' to promote the theme of 'home for life' (Kelly, 2001, p. 57). It is claimed that such housing enables greater mobility through larger space, better standards, planning and fixtures; while locating such housing in accessible areas will also improve a feeling of neighbourhood community. One of the criteria, for example, inside the home is space for a wheelchair to turn in all ground floor rooms, the sitting room to be at entrance level and sufficient space downstairs for a bed or the conversion of a room into a bedroom. Contrary to the universal myth that all older people could downsize in later life, many older people will need as much space as earlier in their lives to maintain their lifestyles (Appleton, 2002).

2 For existing old homes, 'Care and Repair' or 'Staying Put' schemes have been initiated, although there has been criticism about the delay in work to get the home in a good state and quality suitable for the older person rather than meeting regulations (Allen et al., 1997). Re-sale is an issue with many owners in terms of whether they will be able to market a property with a stair lift and other adaptations.

3 Smart homes where technology has been installed to facilitate automation and user-initiated communication emerged in the 1980s to be used by people with mobility problems or sensory impairments as well as communication problems. Such examples include social alarms, automatic lighting, temperature-monitoring devices and medicine monitoring. Movement activated technology using Passive Intra Red devices (switching lights on and off automatically in response to movement) has proved to have considerable potential for people with dementia. Although older people are able to use and adapt to a wide range of technologies

(Appleton, 1999), there are issues of intrusiveness and lifestyle monitoring (Fisk, 1996), for example, through closed-circuit television. There is, however, little evidence to support fears that such monitoring may completely reduce the need for personal contact.

The circumstances of older people who are vulnerable to homelessness or who are homeless are generally under-recognised. The UK Coalition on Older Homelessness 2004 (www.olderhomelessness.org.uk/) defines older homeless people as 'those who are 50 plus and are sleeping rough or living in appropriate temporary accommodation, or are at risk of homelessness'. Warnes and Crane (2000) differentiate between 'official' homeless older people and the 'unofficial' or single homeless population. Official figures suggest that between 4000 and 5000 older people in England lose their homes each year. However, there is a lack of comprehensive statistical evidence showing the true extent of the situation. Help the Aged (2003) estimates that approximately 21 000 people are living in inappropriate hostel accommodation. Help the Aged have combined these figures with the numbers of older people who had referred themselves to bed and breakfast in the country (approximately 27 000) and suggest that an estimate of homelessness among older people in Great Britain resides in the region of 48 000. Warnes and Crane highlight a need for a dedicated service provision for older homeless people. They argue: 'Even when there is a full spectrum of all-age homeless services, providing a pathway from the streets to independent housing, they are unlikely to meet all the needs of older and long-term homeless people' (2000, p. 172). Dedicated services should focus attention on, for example, outreach, rehabilitation and resettlement.

How older people use and perceive spaces in their communities is crucial, however, for their quality of life. A study by Scharf et al. (2002) illustrates the significance of environment, indicating that older people who live in deprived neighbourhoods are more vulnerable to crime than those living in other neighbourhoods. Of the people participating in their survey, 40 per cent had been victims of one or more types of crime in the two years prior to the interview. While crime surveys repeatedly show that older people are relatively unlikely to be victims of crime, their study showed otherwise, particularly for ethnic minorities. Vulnerability to crime is linked to poverty and social inequality as many studies over the years have suggested (Hough, 1995; Silverman and Della-Giustina, 2001; Scharf et al., 2002).

Older people's perceptions of place were also affected by their experience of crime. Lower levels of satisfaction were reported with their neighbourhood among those reported as victims of crime. Neighbourhood satisfaction is also linked to older people's sense of identity. Dissatisfaction with place can translate into a loss of identity and reduced quality of life for older people.

Transportation in terms of walking, driving and use of the public transport system are crucial issues for many older people. Older people can be excluded from transport systems: financially, temporally (unable to get to activities at night); personally and spatially (unable to get to destinations). The goal of transport policy should be to offer all members of society safe, satisfactory and environmentally friendly transportation resources at the lowest possible socio-economic cost, while at the same time integrating people with functional impairments into all parts of society. To make public transport attractive, it must be adapted to the needs of travellers. The design of public transport must proceed from a holistic perspective and presuppose that people have very different needs and preferences when they travel. This implies a demand for high trip frequency, efficiency and good information about travel options, combined with high level service and an accessible outdoor environment with short distances to bus stops and train stations.

Older people, however, use private transport and this is likely to increase, as women in the next generation are more likely to be driving than the current generation of 80-year-olds. Many drivers over 70 experience problems with driving because of physical changes – in vision, ability to detect messages among the clutter on the road – and do not have a quick response time. Yet older people over 75 have fewer crashes per number of licensed drivers (OECD, 2001). Improved sign maintenance, illumination, better 'cat's eyes' and better warnings of crossroads as well as better vehicle design can assist in this respect. Relinquishing driving can be difficult for all sorts of reasons as mentioned earlier if older people are located in remote areas.

Living arrangements

The theme of housing and community raises the issue of living arrangements in general. The determinants of living arrangements are demographic factors (level of childlessness, number of children, trends in marriage and divorce and mortality levels); characteristics of older people (health, education and income); cultural contexts (values); policy (availability of social care); characteristics of family networks (size, age, marital status, income and education) (Tomassini et al., 2003).

Considerable changes have taken place in the living arrangements of older people in the past century. There has been a marked decline in 'complex households' with a corresponding move to single or solo living or living with one other, generally a spouse. Higher proportions of never-married, divorced and childless people than before will require support and living arrangements in old age. Co-residence may have declined as 'intimacy at a distance' has grown with better communication (Grundy, 1999). This may be true for even close relationships such as children.

Care homes

The history of residential care has been well documented (Means and Smith, 1985, 1998; Phillips, 1992; Means et al., 2003). In 2001 there were 341 000 places in residential care homes in the independent and public sectors, mainly for older people. Profiles of such older people show a greater degree of disability and dependency in 2004 than in 1990. Flexibility and choice have been increasing themes in the discussion of residential care, along with attempts to create a 'homely' environment. The most sensitive debates, however, have been over how such care can be financed, with the setting up of the Royal Commission on Long Term Care in 1997 (Sutherland Report, 1999) and the quality and standards that can be expected in such provision. A discussion of the process of admission to care can be found in Chapter 2.

Social relationships

Members of the same cohort have much in common as they have continuity with the past, particularly in terms of global historical events, for example, the Second World War will be a reference point for many current 90-year-olds. In terms of intimate relations, then, the marital relationship is one of peers. Married women are more likely to have a confidant outside the family than men. For men they are more likely to say it is their wife; for women it is likely to be a same-sex friend.

Intergenerational relationships can consist of a number of relationships – daughter, son and grandchildren. Active grandparenting can be a role of choice as it is a relationship not based on rights and obligations but on voluntary and personal involvement. The role has been made more of an ambiguous one as divorce and remarriage increase. However, in such situations grandparents can provide stability and continuity with the past. One of the key areas for social workers is to assess the quality of such relationships as informal care plays a crucial role in supporting older people (see Chapter 2).

Social support

In studies of the family and the community life of older people, the role of the family in supporting older people is central (Wenger, 1984; Phillipson et al., 2001). Similarly, older people themselves play significant reciprocal roles within their families, spanning among other things, caregiving, financial and emotional support. Alongside family, friends are also important, particularly for those without family (Phillipson et al., 2001). In communities they also play important roles as citizens or volunteers. When older people are asked about who is important in their lives, family and friends are rated highly; less so are community members such as vicars; in contrast, formal support services such as health and social workers are inconsequential in the lives of the majority of older people (Phillipson et al., 2001).

Carers

Many older people play supportive roles to grandchildren and children but they are most likely to encounter a social worker when they are in need of support themselves. Such support can come from informal (family, friends), and formal sources (care workers and other professionals). Carers, both in a paid and unpaid capacity, play a pivotal role in the care of older people. Without the support of key social care workers and family carers, the role of the social worker would be impossible.

One of the difficulties in establishing the number of carers in the population is the inconsistency in the definition of a 'carer', both in research studies and in the census. Census figures have varied between 6.8 million (1991) to 5.2 million (in 2001). The current census definition (2001) asks if 'you provide unpaid personal help for a friend or family member with a long-term illness, health problem or disability'. You are asked to include problems which are due to old age. Personal help is defined as including help with basic tasks such as feeding or dressing. Unpaid carers, generally spouses, other family members, friends and others in the community are generally designated under the term 'informal carer' although this is misleading as there is little that is 'informal' about this role. On the other hand, those grouped under 'formal' carers are paid and seen as part of the low-waged, low-skilled social care workforce. This group will be discussed later in Chapter 2.

Since the early 1980s there has been a growing literature on carers of older people. The plight of carers was first highlighted in the feminist literature of the time with an emphasis on the burdens and stresses placed on 'informal' carers, predominantly female and married (Finch and Groves, 1983; Lewis and Meredith, 1988). The profile of carers is, however, far from the stereotype of the 1980s as research has disaggregated the type of carer, nature of care, gender and the situations faced by carers.

The majority of carers under 65 are women. The difference is most marked in the 45–64 age group where 27 per cent of women compared with 19 per cent of men are carers (ONS, 2003). Although the overall impression is that it is predominantly women reciprocating in the care role, men are increasingly playing a role in the care relationship (Fisher, 1994; Arber et al., 2003). Overall, 58 per cent of carers in Britain are women; 42 per cent are men. One in four carers is between 45 and 64 and can face the difficulties of juggling home life, care and work. Carers UK claim there are 4 million people combining work with informal care for another adult (Howard, 2002).

Caregiving can stretch across all age groups. Loss of education can be another factor faced by 'young carers' looking after disabled parents (Becker, et al., 1998). Increasingly, the issues faced by older carers looking after their spouse raise particular issues of interdependency. Similarly, an older parent caring for an adult with a learning disability is an issue as more people with a learning disability are surviving into old age (Walker and Walker, 1998).

Further differentiation can be made in terms of the nature of the task. Women are more likely to help with personal care tasks than men who are more likely to be involved in taking the older person out or managing their finances. Some 60 per cent of carers are looking after someone with a physical disability; 7 per cent are looking after someone with a mental health problem. This differentiation will lead to potentially different kinds of stress for carers and different experiences of care. In one study of carers of adults with learning disabilities, 80 per cent of carers reported levels of stress indicative of psychiatric problems. This was associated with material disadvantage, lack of informal support, and low take-up of services due in part to lack of information, staff with inappropriate language skills and general neglect of religious and cultural needs in assessment (Haton et al., 1998).

Providing care is also time-consuming with 1.7 million carers devoting at least 20 hours a week to caring and 855 000 of these spending over 50 hours in this role. Consequently, the impact on carers' employment can be severe. In the Carers UK survey (Howard, 2002) around six out of ten carers had given up work to provide care. The consequences of the loss of income and pension accruement for women to provide security in their own old age can therefore be significant (Evandrou and Glaser, 2003).

The location of care also impacts on the type and frequency of care provision. The majority of carers (over two-thirds) provide care to someone who lives in a separate household. A number of studies illustrate the difficulties where distance between home, work and the care recipient – with 30 minutes travelling time being the cut-off point for providing daily personal care (Phillips et al., 2003).

One of the major limitations of earlier definitions of 'care' was the emphasis on 'instrumental care' – 'doing for' or 'doing with' tasks often to the exclusion of emotional caring. Nolan et al. (1998) highlight the stress of this kind of care long before caring is 'seen' and describes this as anticipatory care, based on anticipated future need. Eligibility for services, however, has long been associated with the demonstration of 'hands on' care; it ignores the stresses carers may face emotionally, as they 'monitor from a distance'.

There are a number of further factors in caregiving impacting on the experiences for both carer and care recipient, such as the history of the past relationship and the quality of that relationship (the relationship may be based on years of abuse between father and child, with the roles of abuser and abused now reversed); prognosis and trajectory of the illness or condition requiring care and the carer's attitude (Nolan et al., 1998).

Increasingly, we have an extensive body of knowledge from both carers' accounts and quantitative information about what it is to be engaged in informal care. Financial costs can stem from a loss of income in addition to the increased costs from care such as incontinence aids; physical costs arise through risks of personal injury in lifting, fatigue and stress; mental and emotional costs and social costs through isolation and potential household conflict. Such problems may be appraised as stress factors by carers. As Nolan et al. (1996) illustrate, however, the rewards and satisfactions of caregiving are rarely addressed. They can exist, however, in terms of interpersonal factors (such as satisfaction derived from meeting the need for nurturing and care; feeling that they are able to repay and reciprocate for the caring done by the person needing care in the past) and intrapersonal factors (such as a sense of fulfilment in helping another or religious beliefs in caring). Satisfaction in a number of studies referenced above is associated with a good past history in the relationship and the attitude of the carer to their caring role.

Care is found in a variety of situations and relationships. Carers are the linchpin of sustaining older people in the community. Older people themselves value and prefer a mixture of care from both family and friends and from care workers (Daatland and Herlofson, 2003). The dynamics of care are, however, changing with different relationships emerging, e.g. lesbian and gay care relationships and friends talking on more care tasks, together with different expectations of who should provide care in the future.

All the above factors will play a role in the quality of life of older people. In the past five years there have been a number of research studies addressing this issue (www.shef.ac.uk/uni/projects/gop 2003). Assessing the quality of life and understanding the factors involved in this is an essential skill for social workers.

Quality of life

The lifecourse is central to any understanding of ageing, as this chapter has outlined. The individual experience of ageing will be determined by the cultural, economic, clinical, and social factors over a lifetime. Diversity in quality of life is a dominant theme therefore in old age. It is the subjective evaluation of objective living conditions that has an impact on people's behaviour.

Research shows that, in particular, health, income and education have a strong impact on most dimensions of subjective quality of life (Tesch-Roemer et al., 2003). This is not to say that objective conditions do not play a significant part. Health, income and wealth, age and gender all correlate to satisfaction in old age (Mannell and Dupuis, 1996). The influence of social networks and social support characteristics is also vital in subjective well-being. Marital status is important in this respect with older married men having higher levels of satisfaction compared to non-married men and married women; similarly, having children also has an impact.

Conclusion: implications for social work

The diverse situations and heterogeneity of older people provide a backdrop to social work. It is crucial to acknowledge the diversity in social, cultural, economic, financial, political, gender, generational and ethnic circumstances among others. This collage of circumstances and experience also has a temporal dimension as present circumstances are shaped by a lifetime of events, relationships, economic and social circumstances as well as class, gender, ethnicity, race and location.

Social workers, however, will meet older people from all lifestyles through their personal and professional relationships yet they are more likely to work with those who experience poverty, ill health, depression, dementia, and traumas in earlier years, along with those in greatest need. It is imperative that social workers place their work in context and do not view older people from a negative and ageist perspective.

As we learn more about the situation of older people, this becomes an exciting time for those engaged in practice with older people. Future cohorts may bring very different agendas as living arrangements, expectations and aspirations, economic and societal circumstances change.

Given that most older people do not need a social worker or come into contact with them, why is social work with older people important? What are the reasons for social work and what is the remit of the social worker in the lives of older people? Chapter 2 turns to why social work has a role to play in the lives of older people.

putting it into practice

Activity 1

Think about an older person you know. How does their experience differ from yours? How have gender, class, income, culture and location influenced their experiences in later life? You may find it helpful to interview them about significant life events and their experience of later life.

Activity 2

Investigate a cross-section of newspapers covering the main news items of the week. To what extent are older people evident in the news? What images and situations are portrayed in the media? How can these images be challenged or promoted?

Activity 3

What differences are there in the experiences of men and women in old age? To what extent do such differences exist for older people in other countries? You may like to consider ageing in Africa, China or Iceland!

further reading

Ageing and Society http://titles.cambridge.org/journals/journal

Bernard, M. and Phillips, J. (eds) (1998) *The Social Policy of Old Age*. Centre for Policy on Ageing, London.

Walker, A. (2003) *Growing Older: Quality of Life in Older Age*. Open University Press, Buckingham shire.

2 | The case for social work with older people

Chapter 1 outlined the diverse experiences of later life and the importance for social workers to understand the context in which ageing takes place. Most people do not need or come into contact with a social worker and live their lives without intervention from social services. However, a minority of older people and their carers will need to draw on social work skills. This chapter outlines the reasons for social work with older people, such as transitions associated with bereavement, taking on a caregiving role or admission to residential care which may pose difficulties.

Social workers also need to understand why they practise in particular ways and the chapter concludes by exploring frameworks for social work with older people, such as the importance of theory, knowledge-based practice and reflexivity. Just as important is the legislative, policy and organisational context which is further discussed in Chapter 3.

Older people and personal social services

The myth that ageing is inevitably a period of decline was challenged in Chapter 1. The need for personal social services in older age is by no means inevitable and relatively few older people use social services. Data from the General Household Survey 2001 (Walkes et al., 2003) suggested that overall, 3 per cent of men and 5 per cent of women aged 65 and over were receiving local authority (council) home care services. Some 9 per cent of men and 12 per cent of women aged 65 and over received private home care. However, people aged 85 and over were more likely to receive personal social services of all types than any other age group (ONS, 2001b). In 2001, 28 per cent of older people aged 85 and over received private home care and 18 per cent received local authority home care services. Even though this constitutes a significant increase when compared to other parts of the lifecourse, it is still the case that over 50 per cent of people aged 85 and over did not receive any form of home care support. This is partly because many older people remain in good health, or maintain their abilities to undertake their usual roles and responsibilities. It is also partly explained by the fact that spouses, family members and friends may provide care and support and do not seek the help of personal social services. Eligibility criteria and Fair Access to Care policies (see Chapter 3) in local councils mean that older people in the greatest and most pressing need will receive services and so other older people, who perhaps experience some degree of difficulty, but are not eligible for services, look elsewhere to meet those needs, or they go unmet.

There is no established age at which older people are entitled to 'community care' services. Indeed, there is a duty upon local authorities (councils) to assess an adult who has an 'appearance of need' regardless of their age under Section 47 of the *National Health Service and Community Care Act* (WMSO, 1990b). Nevertheless, many local councils in the past operated age-based criteria for services with younger people entitled to resources that older people may not have received. For example, younger people with disabilities were allocated greater financial support for respite care than older people. The *National Service Framework for Older People* (DoH, 2001b), however, has changed this state of affairs. Given that a minority of older people receive social services and social work, what are the reasons for social work with older people?

Reasons for social work

Physical frailty

Social workers are likely to meet older people who are viewed as 'frail', through both physical disability and/or cognitive impairment. In such situations, social workers and older people, along with others, will need to make judgements about needs, strengths and resources as well as risks, danger, and the availability of informal support. One of the key policy objectives (voiced in the White Paper, *Growing Older*) since the late 1980s has been to keep older people at home 'for as long as possible', 'care in the community increasingly meaning care by the community' (DHSS,

1981, p. 3). This aspiration is often coupled with professional goals to maintain independence, autonomy and to promote self-determination. Yet, the complexity of some older people's needs may lead to difficult and painful decisions about the ability of the elderly person to manage at home with or without formal support. There is also an important debate about the value that is placed on the concept of autonomy and the consequences for older people who may be dependent upon formal services. A study of ageing, built on the concept of 'successful' ageing (Rowe and Kahn, 1998) highlights the importance of positive health and active participation in life (see Chapter 1). It focuses on individuals having the power to achieve a desirable state. However, Holstein and Minkler (2003) highlight the potential dangers for ageing women, for example:

● The very term 'successful' implies that the other side of the coin is 'failure'.
● Lifecourse experience and the impact of structural oppression and disadvantage are not considered.
● Further, the concept does not leave much possibility for an older person who, for example, uses a wheelchair, to successfully age on their own terms and in their own way.
● Even visible oldness signifies failure or at best, 'usual ageing'. They argue: 'When norms consider frailty and disability as reflections of failure, they reinforce cultural fears of bodily suffering (and thus of people who are old) and promote inadequate policy responses' (2003, p. 702) and 'The tyranny of youth-preserving technologies and lifestyles that demand more and more time and money hinders a respectful attitude toward old age. How can we respect age if we do everything in our power to deny it?' (2003, p. 795).

Many people will enter old age living with long-term disability. Optimistically, evidence given to the Royal Commission on Long Term Care suggests that 'factors which are causing us to live longer (better diet, healthier lifestyles, improved housing conditions) are also resulting in extra years of life being free from severe disability' (Sutherland Report, 1999, para 2.23), but social workers are likely to work with people who have spent years in poor health. The major causes of chronic illness and disability in later life are many, such as cardiovascular diseases (stroke and coronary heart disease), cancers, arthritis and osteoporosis, degenerative diseases causing hearing and visual loss and dementia. It is important for social workers to be fully informed on the causes of such diseases, their prognoses and preventative strategies in place to assist older people with decision-making. For example, taking osteoporosis (increasing porousness of the bone), in the UK, there are 600 000 hip fractures annually due to osteoporosis; the consequences can mean life-long disability and can act as a trigger for admission into residential care. Less than 50 per cent of all hip fracture patients return home following surgery (Age Concern, 2000). Rehabilitation strategies involving health and social care 'experts' are crucial if people are to maintain independence.

Cognitive impairment

It is inevitable that social work with older people will involve working with people with dementia (diagnosed) or with cognitive impairments that are not diagnosed. Chapter 1 highlighted the fact that depression is a common and often under-diagnosed experience for older people. Social workers in this context must have the skills to work positively with older people who may be experiencing memory difficulties, communication needs, anxiety and fear. Judgements and decisions are likely to be made more complex by issues such as the person's ability to make informed decisions; by issues of risk and danger and the availability of support and helping networks. As well as providing interventions and support to directly assist a person with dementia (see Chapter 5), there is a need to provide practical advice and help to those people providing informal care and support to older people with dementia, depression and other conditions.

Social work with people with dementia and their families is no different in focus but is characterised by a constant battle against negative stereotypes and an exceptionally high emotional content. Huge advances have been made in our understanding of the bio-psychosocial aspects of dementia which, if anything, have made the job more challenging. We are now, for example, beginning to understand that we can 'hear the language' of people with advanced dementia and that they often have very sad things to say (Killick and Allan, 2001; Allan, 2001, 2002).

Social work with people with dementia in the more advanced stages needs to be both speedy and closely linked to the input of health care colleagues because of the profound and often sudden impact of changes in health and circumstances. Dehydration, for example, can lead to or can exacerbate an infection. Delirium often occurs and in no time a hospital admission may be required with all the negative consequences that can follow.

Emotional and psychological issues: transitions in mid and later life

Older people may face a range of emotional and psychological issues that they require help and support to manage. Social workers frequently meet older people who, for example, experience depression or low morale because of disability and illness; who are bereaved or facing loss (either of people or loss associated with their own illness); who experience a shrinking network as a result of successive bereavements; who are facing death or are dying. Such changes can occur at any stage in the lifecourse but are more commonly associated with older age.

George (1982) argues that change can be viewed as transition rather than crisis in old age. Transitions in mid and later life are often dependent on earlier life events around marriage, childbearing and work. For others, past trauma, such as child or domestic abuse, can become significant in how ageing and later life are approached (Hunt et al., 1997). As Hunt et al. note in *Past Trauma in Later Life*, social workers come across instances of unresolved trauma as part of their routine work with older people.

Whether social workers become involved in the transition points in people's lives depends on how the individual and their support network cope with the change. For many, the pain of trauma may have lain dormant until old age, only to be expressed possibly though exhibiting 'difficult' behaviour in residential care. This is not to conclude that past trauma cannot be worked with successfully (Hunt et al., 1997). Most situations that social workers come across will be different from their own experiences and this is particularly true for those experiencing current trauma. Five transitions applied to ageing are discussed below: retirement; caregiving, admission to residential care, bereavement and death and dying, with a view to exploring the social work role in each.

Redundancy and the transition to retirement

Retirement, whatever it brings, can be the gateway to a long and significant period in people's lives, particularly for people who are able and have taken advantage of early retirement from paid work. Retirement is a western industrial phenomenon, experienced by men in Britain in 2004 at 65 and women at 60, although this is subject to changes earlier or later depending on society's needs. According to Labour Market Trends 2003, just over 1 per cent of the labour force are people over retirement age (Dixon, 2003). Whereas the early literature on retirement viewed work and retirement as a man's domain, increasingly women are more likely to experience retirement. The male breadwinner model, of the man as sole or main earner in the household no longer holds true for many families, with women increasingly in part-time jobs (Crompton, 1999). The public–private spheres of home and workplace are also no longer gender-specific with women's time being spent in the public domain of the workplace. However, the low level of women's earnings and the consequent inability to make long-term financial plans have severe consequences for them in later life. For women, the role as worker is also an important feature of their identity, particularly for those without a partner (Bernard et al., 1995). Many women will face divorce and demand for informal care, both of which have an impact on the financial security of women in old age.

Research on retirement illustrates the importance of being prepared (Phillipson, 1993). Quality of life research shows that health and income are significant factors in later life quality and hence planning for retirement becomes a crucial factor, as discussed in Chapter 1 (Tesch-Roemer et al., 2003).

Early studies on retirement highlight the fact that it may be the first period of time that couples have a sustained period together. It may be a testing time for relationships. Some people may have found that the focus of their lives was on their children and not themselves and renegotiating the pattern of life together for many years to come can cause tensions within marriages. Retirement, particularly if alongside ill health or caregiving (Ray, 2000a, 2000b), can be stressful, particularly if the latter is unexpected. Social workers need to be aware of this time in someone's life and may need to intervene if this is a time of crisis.

Caregiving

Caring can occur at any age, although the 'structural potential' (the likelihood of caring in relation to position in society) for caregiving increases with age (Martin-Mathews and Keefe, 1995). Many people who dream of a leisurely retirement may be unexpectedly taking on the role of carer for elderly parents or for their spouse as they age. Arber and Ginn (1991) first demonstrated, in their reanalysis of the General Household Survey, the contribution of older people in care provision, amounting to 35 per cent of the total volume of informal care to people aged 65 or over and nearly 50 per cent of co-resident care of older men and women. Co-resident spouse care is the predominant care situation in later life yet their significant contribution is often overlooked. Their relative invisibility, in comparison with caregivers in other parts of the lifecourse, may serve to reinforce the myth that very old women and men are inevitably a burden both on their family members and the state. Based on available evidence, spouse care is likely to remain the most reliable and predictable form of informal care (Finch, 1995). Research has also demonstrated the likelihood for spouse care to create conditions for high and intensive forms of care-giving as it is not delimited by, for example, living in separate households and is likely to be reinforced by notions of marital obligation, duty and responsibility. This observation highlights the fact that, care-giving is not, as is often implied in care-giving research, a unified and unproblematic concept (Ray 2000a, 2000b).

Chapter 1 highlighted the stresses and compensations that carers face and social workers need to be perceptive to the needs of carers if they are to intervene appropriately. The assessment of carers is discussed in Chapter 5.

A further transition may occur in mid and later life for carers of disabled adults. The stereotypical picture of a carer is the notion of a daughter or son providing care for a parent but increasingly there will be ageing parents of people with a learning disability. In one study (McGrother et al., 1996), family carers aged 60 and over were responsible for looking after 44 per cent of all adults with a learning disability who were living in a family home. The ability to continue caring, concerns about the future of their son or daughter and about being 'perpetual parents' (Tobin, 1996) are areas where social workers can provide support. Realistic care options need to be discussed with all concerned. Further interventions are discussed by Grant (2001). *Valuing People* (DH, 2001c) sets out to increase the support for carers, particularly for those with complex needs.

Admission to residential care

One of the most painful transitions faced in late old age may be the admission to residential care. For a minority of people each year this is a major transition point. Although this represents a small percentage of the total older population, it is a difficult step for a significant minority and fears of care can pervade the thoughts of those who are at risk of or vulnerable to care, even if they do not ultimately enter institutional care.

Although it is beyond the scope of this book to detail the history of residential and nursing care, the legacy of the past has haunted this form of provision. It can be argued that the critique of residential life in accounts such as *The Last Refuge* (Townsend, 1962) had lasting damage on the image of care, which still remains and which led to a raft of legislation moving away from this form of care to the realisation of 'community care'. However, what was left was a tarnished image of residential care, under-resourced, stigmatised, and contracted out to the private sector.

Prior to the *National Health Service and Community Care Act* (HMSO, 1990b) one of the main tasks of the social worker was to provide a smooth transition to residential care for older people following an assessment of need. Although this remains a key area of work, the focus has become less dominant in the social workers' repertoire of work.

For older people facing this transition admission to care can be traumatic. Older people will have experienced multiple losses as a trigger to admission (both in their social support and physical and/ or mental functioning) and will face loss of their home and uncertainty about making new relationships (Phillips, 1992). The decision to enter care is often not primarily theirs, with the influence of others (GP and relatives) often being paramount. In some situations older people are faced with 'eviction' as residential homes go out of business. The idea of consumer choice is therefore often tokenistic. This is exacerbated by the two-tier system where those with money are able to 'top up' social services payments and extend their choices. Such vulnerability, powerlessness and loss of meaning are characterised by life inside the care home (Casey and Holmes, 1995). Lack of social stimulation, low staff-resident interpersonal interaction, and poor psychological stimulation and outside contact have all been reported (Phillips, 1992; Nolan et al., 1995).

A number of frameworks have been advocated to describe the process of admission to a care home (Jones, 1972; Phillips, 1992; Nolan et al., 1996) and, if planned and anticipated, the transition can be a positive experience. Patterson (1995) highlights emotional support as a key factor in adjustment to a home and it is here that social workers involved in the transition can play a vital role as one of the continuity points between home or hospital and residential care. Social workers will have information pertinent to the decision and an understanding of the process of admission itself and the significance of the event for the person. Throughout the process, social workers should act as advocates, promoting the strengths of the older person. Additionally, they should ensure as care managers that systems work together to provide a 'seamless' transition, for example, between hospital to care home, a route that many older people follow (Phillips and Waterson, 2002).

There is very little research on older people leaving institutions to live in the community; the statistics are too small for quantitative analysis and qualitative accounts are few. There are two areas where social work has a role, however, first, through the relocation of older people with learning disabilities and, second, an increasing issue of the resettlement of older offenders after release from prison. Although this second issue may appear marginal in the reasons for social work, it is an area which is likely to expand as more and longer life sentences are experienced (Phillips, 2004) and is an area which will require the skills of social workers in assessments of social care needs and placements.

Earlier studies looked at how older people have been treated by police and the courts as offenders (Taylor and Parrot, 1988; Thomas and Wall, 1993) yet there has been little work on what happens after prison or while on probation, i.e. what social support and resettlement needs do they have? What peer support exists outside? What family and social relationships continue, particularly for the high number of sex offenders? What is the level and content of the provision of care and what is the role of formal agencies in resettlement, and who pays for their care?

From limited research we know that inequality, homelessness, institutionalisation and a lack of role outside prison can perpetuate and encourage dependency, deny autonomy and can lead to recidivism (Howse, 2003). Prison inmates are destitute, homeless and dependent on the state as they have little entitlement while inside. Ex-prisoners also have families who may find coping with life in their communities difficult. The role of the social worker in following a welfare approach (rather than a justice approach reserved for the probation officer role) will have significance if people are to rebuild their lives and find meaning in their lives.

Bereavement

As people age, grief and loss of friends and family are an inevitable part of life. The experience of widowhood is particularly a female issue, because of gender differences in mortality. The proportion of widows increases with age. Until the 1990s the situation of widowhood was pathologised; widows were portrayed as lonely and isolated, in a period of decline (Chambers, 2000) and dependent on others, with the social work role in the provision of counselling and provision of support services. Such stereotypes have, however, been challenged (Martin-Matthews, 1991). Widowhood is not necessarily a negative experience but for some it can be a new anxiety-provoking and lonely one.

Coping with bereavement depends on personality, social status, education and culture, life experience and expectations of others. Friendship ties take on significance, highlighting the continuities that are present in most people's lives. Looking at the strengths of older people and the resilience they develop to multiple losses over their lifetime is a starting point for social work assessment. For some, the loss of a spouse will be profound but for others it may be a liberating experience. As people live longer, they will increasingly experience the loss of cohort members as well as others younger than themselves.

Living alone in old age can prove an isolating experience for some, particularly if they have moved from living with parents and siblings to marriage and children and have for the first time in their lives had to cope with being alone.

'End of life' issues

Issues around death and dying face everyone yet still present a 'taboo' area in society. The quality of life at the end is, however, an area for social workers to explore to become competent practitioners with older people. The challenge is not to reinforce the stereotype associated between old age and death (Siddell et al., 1998). Some older people will have explored advanced directives, euthanasia, and thought about the refusal of treatment as well as funeral arrangements, wills and other practical arrangements. Issues such as autonomy and control are, however, often difficult to achieve. Palliative care puts the focus on the relief of pain, with support to the family and patient underpinning this work. Most of this specialist work occurs in hospices, yet older people will die of conditions other than just terminal illnesses, such as cancer, in hospital or in residential care, if not their own home. Death and dying are particularly complex when the person has dementia and may be unable to verbally express pain. There is a debate about whether people with dementia understand they are dying and it is at such times that families, the staff and the people themselves will particularly need support.

Social workers therefore need to know how to handle such situations, working with the dying person with honesty and sensitivity. Meaningful communication is possible even in advanced states and this can be beneficial to families and people involved in care. Allaying the fears of the 'patient', the family and being sensitive to their emotional and spiritual needs are crucial. Although this work may predominantly be that of the hospital social worker, social workers in the community are likely to face traumatic situations where dying is an issue as they work with older people with complex problems (for example, suicidal tendencies) and often in complex family situations (where abuse may have occurred).

Substance misuse

Chapter 1 also highlighted the potential to overlook the complex and multiple needs that may be associated with alcohol problems and drug misuse. It is clearly important that social workers challenge their assumptions about older people, for example, that a woman of 85 cannot have an alcohol problem may mean that interventions are inappropriate, misguided and doomed to fail.

Current attitudes among younger people about alcohol and drug taking suggest that the numbers of older people who will develop related problems will be on the increase. A lifetime of abuse will have severe repercussions for later life. Assessing older people and defining their alcohol dependency are difficult issues as the traditional areas in which problems may manifest themselves may not be available, for example, being drunk in a workplace or a public place as older people are more likely to drink at home privately. There may also be age-related losses of memory, difficulty in concentration and behaviour swings which can mask any problem caused by alcohol.

For older people who are dependent on alcohol for a considerable period of time, family and support systems may have withdrawn; for others, it may be the loss of family, work and social status that has led to substance abuse. Social workers have a role to play here in acknowledging the problem and its seriousness to others, directing people to Alcoholics Anonymous and other support groups as well as individual counselling.

Similarly, social workers need to be aware of the potential for iatrogenic illness, particularly in relation to prescribed medication. Older people are the largest consumers of prescribed and over-the-counter medication. Drug dependency develops more rapidly among older people due to the same metabolic factors that contribute to alcohol dependency (McInnis-Dittrich, 2002). Drugs related to relief of pain, depression and insomnia are commonly misused and there is a well-documented issue of people across the lifecourse becoming addicted to 'over-the-counter' pain relief medication. Social workers can help in monitoring medication as part of the assessment process and should work with health professionals.

Suicide among older people is another area of concern for social workers. Valuing human life is a key area of work and this area, often neglected in practice, should be addressed as seriously as it is among other age groups. Suicide is more common among men. Risk factors include depression, often accompanied by drug and alcohol misuse, physical illness and recent bereavement or loss.

It is important for social workers to be proactive in these situations, both working on short-term solutions (ensuring there are no harmful stockpiles of tablets) as well as longer term solutions (such as a referral for pain management).

Risk and protection

During the 1990s terminology focused on 'vulnerable' older people and elder abuse became an issue on the social work agenda. Since this time there have been a number of research studies, books and chapters written on social work and elder abuse (Hughes, 1995; Bennet et al., 1997). Much of the debate has been on defining abuse and measuring its incidence and prevalence (Decalmer and Glendenning, 1993). Increasingly procedural guidelines have appeared such as the *No Secrets* (DoH, 2000) which assist in defining the role of the social worker (see Chapters 5 and 6). The dilemmas in identifying and responding to this illustrate the complexity of social work along with the importance of building a relationship with older people to agree on what forms of action should be taken.

Challenging ageism

Increasingly as people grow older, one of the pervading experiences faced is that of ageism (Bytheway, 1995). This is one of the key experiences which social workers face in working with older people. Negative stereotypes of older people are found everywhere, including social work practice. One example can be found when comparing the media coverage and social work involvement when an older person is abused and dies as a result, compared to a child in the same situation (for examples, see Butler and Drakeford, 2003). Counter to this is the notion of 'active ageing' (Rowe and Kahn, 1998) with the emphasis on activity and positive ageing, which can further marginalise those who are already dependent and frail.

The diversity in the older population illustrated in Chapter 1 undoubtedly poses challenges for social workers. A 'one size fits all approach' to social work and care management cannot be adequate in the context of such diversity. Complex life circumstances experienced by an older service user add further layers of intricacy to a social worker's own involvement and, indeed, her or his involvement with other agencies. This again highlights the importance of providing interventions which go beyond the simple provision of 'off the peg' services. Social workers should do the following:

● Tailor services to individual need and actively seek to enable an older person to build on their strengths, abilities and resources rather than focusing on problems, dysfunctions and pathologies. Looking at the strengths of older people and the resilience they develop to multiple losses over their lifetime is a starting point for social work assessment.

- Plan and provide interventions aimed at alleviating the difficulties associated with the context and based on the needs and aspirations of the older person (for example, enabling an older person to talk about their bereavement and facilitate communication).
- Realise the potential for change in older people in terms of physical, mental and emotional health. Older people can also be resilient in the face of severe difficulties.
- Evaluate the outcomes of services and interventions; did your interventions do what they set out to do? Has the older person achieved goals and outcomes that were important and relevant to him/her? In what way has there been change, and to what extent?
- Mediate and advocate for older people (for example, in respect of allocating resources and services; helping an older person attend a case conference or review meeting).

These points are expanded in our chapter on care planning, monitoring and intervention.

Frameworks for understanding social work with older people

Social workers, if they are to be professional practitioners, need to be equipped with a grounding in gerontological and social work theory, an ability to draw on research to inform their practice as well as be able to reflect on their own work.

Gerontological theory

To practise successfully social workers should have theoretical knowledge of the areas they are working in. Gerontological theory and social work theory are two key areas to consider in relation to an appropriate knowledge base for social work with older people. Gerontology has been broadly defined as the study of ageing from biological, psychological and social perspectives; it is a multi-disciplinary subject. In the UK it has traditionally reflected the disciplines of sociology and social policy, but increasingly history, anthropology, economic and psychological perspectives are influencing the discipline.

Theory development in gerontology has reflected its traditional background with disengagement theory (Cumming and Henry, 1961), role theory and activity theory (Havighurst and Albrecht,

1953), modernisation theory (Cowgill and Holmes, 1972) and continuity theory (Atchley, 1989) coming from sociology. These early (in the history of gerontology) or 'first generation' theories (Bengtson et al., 1997) were all based on the continuity or disconti- nuity between different phases of life, that is, older people had to respond by acknowledging a withdrawal in life, by taking on new roles or the maintenance of activities. Exchange theory also stressed a discontinuity in terms of the loss of power from older to younger generations. Many of these earlier theories were driven by policy concerns of the 'burden' of an ageing population and pathol- ogised older people.

More recent theoretical development (since 1975) can be significant for social work in helping us to understand problems and provide us with explanations. Unlike the first (1949–69) and 'second-generation' theories (1970–85), which attempted an all-encompassing 'theory of ageing,' the 'third generation' have provided multiple theories and several different lenses with which to look at the world of ageing.

The perspective which critiques the existing frameworks and institutions of ageing is called a critical gerontology. Within this there are a number of approaches – the political economy of ageing and feminist gerontology for example. The political economy perspective has brought a significant change in the perception regarding old age. It attempts to explain how the interaction of economic and political forces determine how social resources are allocated and how variations in treatments and status of elderly people can be understood in examining public policies, economic trends and social structural factors. The 'ageing enterprise' (Estes, 1979) challenged the view that growing older was dominated by decline. Old age was socially constructed (Phillipson, 1982).

One of the critiques of this theoretical approach is that it treated older people as passive recipients of their social world, without agency to act. This was addressed by narrative and biographical approaches which placed an emphasis on the notion of ageing as 'lived experience' and the meaning of growing old (Moody, 1988; Gubrium, 1993). Critical to these perspectives was also the issue of reflexivity.

Reflexivity

One of the key elements in social work is 'use of self'. Being reflective and self-critical of one's practice is necessary. All social workers will have (if they live long lives), the experience of ageing. Many will have had relationships with grandparents. Knowing why they interpret and what knowledge and experience they draw on and what they leave out in their analysis of situations are necessary. It is important for social workers to ask the question: what impact has social work on my understanding of my own ageing? What prejudices do I bring to the work (Phillips, 1996, 2003)?

Social work theories

The application of appropriate theory to practice is vital if older people are to be given a quality service and if social workers are to have any understanding of why they are operating the way they are. There are a number of texts on social work theory which will be of use (Adams et al., 1998). Throughout this book we draw on examples of task-focused, person-centred approaches, biography and cognitive behaviour therapy. Increasingly, knowledge and theory from one area of social work are applied to other areas, for example, the use of attachment theory (used primarily with early years) to look at the responses to bereavement (Machin, 2001) and to later life filial relationships (Shemmings, 2004).

Biographical approaches illustrate the utility of bringing together gerontological and social work theories. Our biographies are unique to us and represent the totality of our experience in the context of our lifecourse. What purpose might biography have in relation to social work with older people?

- Biography can highlight that each older person is unique and will bring their own interpretations to their experiences; this provides information, for example, about the ways in which older people might approach the management of change.
- A detailed biography can explore continuities and coherences in the person's life and the experience and impact of discontinuity.
- It also enables us to see the ways in which older people construct their identities: what is important to the older person?; what does an older person wish to retain as continuity and how do they cope with the loss of important aspects of their lives?

In the context of assessment, the benefits to users will be many. The social worker is able to elicit older people's attitudes; to understand family relationships; to find out about relationships between carers and the older person and to determine what kinds of help would be unacceptable. Additionally, they will be able to relate to and understand how people might be labelled 'difficult'; to learn how people coped with past difficulties and hardship; and to assess how people might react and be helped effectively in some future crisis. The use of biography is discussed in the context of assessment in Chapter 5. Biographical approaches in direct work are also commonly undertaken with older people, for example, life review and reminiscence work. The role of biography in direct work with older people is reviewed in Chapter 6.

Knowledge-based practice

Practice should be informed by research, practitioner wisdom and service user perspectives, collectively termed 'knowledge-based practice'. Knowledge or evidence-based practice may be defined as 'the conscientious, explicit and judicious use of current best evidence in making decisions regarding the welfare of those in need of social services' (Sheldon and MacDonald, 1999, p. 4). This means that there is an onus on workers to keep up to date with research findings and with appropriate support, to be able to evaluate research and make sound decisions about its quality. There are, after all, potential dangers in changing practice or investing resource in adopting new practices when the research on which the change is based is poorly designed. This is, at present, one of the difficulties in adopting knowledge-based practice in social care; good quality, reliable research is not always available. Sheldon and MacDonald argue that, too often, research has relied on inadequate samples, flawed methodology and, indeed, the application of an inappropriate research method to investigate the question at hand. Not surprisingly, social care research which focuses on 'what works' in social work with older people, is often sparse. There is a need to continue developing the knowledge base through good quality research and practitioners have a role in this at a number of levels. For example:

- discussing current research in social work lectures, team meetings, supervision sessions, practice teaching meetings
- developing skills in evaluating the quality of research and assessing how appropriate the research method is for the research questions being addressed

- knowing the strategies that are in place in your own area of work for understanding research-based evidence
- making sure that practitioners evaluate carefully your own practice and interventions.

Knowledge-based practice has a number of important functions. For example, it may result in significant change to strategic planning of service development. Morbey et al. (2001) highlighted the potential contributions of Home Improvement Agencies (HIAs) to the role of social work with older people. Together with assistive technology, input from HIAs can provide creative options for older people with dementia who might otherwise be at risk of admission to a care home. The authors highlight the importance of social work practitioners mapping the availability of such resources in their location.

Research may highlight what older service users value in service delivery and, indeed, provide insights into the ways in which older people define and experience need. Research, for example, has provided important insights into the experience of older people with dementia and outcomes of community care (Bamford and Bruce, 2000). A key outcome, relatively neglected in previous work, was maximising a sense of autonomy.

Finally, we can understand the social work response to older people by examining legislation and policy and this is addressed in the next chapter.

Conclusion

This chapter has attempted to put age into context, as well as define and address the issues of ageing within contemporary Britain. Opportunities are presented by an ageing society with new lifestyles, careers and work locations emerging, an emphasis on 'active ageing' and on intergenerational issues. For social workers it is crucial to understand this potential of ageing as their experiences will, by definition of their role, be concentrated on frail older people and their carers, who face such problems that they are forced to seek help from formal sources. Such problems may be linked to transitions and crises such as bereavement or substance misuse. To make sense of the situation of older people, social workers need to have knowledge of theory, research, policy and legislation, as well as the ability to reflect on their own practice. All these factors are crucial in framing social work with older people. Social workers are, however, agents of the state and their role is defined by legislation and policy. Before moving on to Part II of this book, on practice issues, we address both the legislative and organisational policy context under which social work operates. This poses different challenges and opportunities for social workers.

putting it into practice

Activity 1

Think about other life transitions that may affect older people. These may not necessarily be age-related and may not involve a need for social work.

Activity 2

What clues would you look for to assess whether an older person is at risk of emotional abuse? Or has suicidal tendencies? What other agencies would you work with?

Activity 3

What particular stresses face carers looking after older people with a mental health problem or a learning disability? Explore the literature to find out how many older people over the age of 60 have a learning disability and how many older people over 80 are carers for children with a learning disability. Think about the social work role.

Further reading

Crawford, K. and Walker, J. (2004) *Social Work with Older People*. Learning Matters, Exeter.

McInnis-Dittrich, K. (2002) *Social Work with Elders: A Biopsychosocial Approach to Assessment and Intervention*. Allyn and Bacon, Boston.

Neysmith, S. (ed.) (1999) *Critical Issues for Future Social Work Practice with Ageing Persons*. Columbia University Press, New York.

Also check out the Social Care Institute of Excellence Website: www.scie.org.uk

3 | The policy and organisational context of social work with older people

Adult welfare services have been dominated in the past decade by the reorganisation of provision to care management processes and practices and underpinned by the *National Health Service and Community Care Act* (HMSO, 1990b). It is important for social workers to understand the principles underpinning this pivotal piece of legislation and the subsequent development of services to older people. Unlike the *Children Act* (1990), the *National Health Service and Community Care Act 1990* s.47 (hereafter referred to as *NHSCCA*) did not provide a unified and coherent system for adult care services but instead, 'exists in conjunction with pre-existing duties and responsibilities and introduces changes in structure and the ways in which social care is provided rather than in substance' (Brammer, 2003, p. 304). We begin this chapter looking at these pre-existing duties and responsibilities, by reviewing the major legislation and policy in this area up to the 1990 Act. We then move on to briefly look at the modernisation of social services and some of the key areas of change in work with older people. This is followed by a discussion of the changing role of the social worker. As stated in Chapter 2, it is policy and legislation that define and legitimise the roles and tasks of social workers with older people. Social care is constantly changing and it is important for social workers to keep up to date on legislative changes and their implication for social work.

The history of welfare services for older people

The policy overview highlights the main policy developments culminating in the *NHS and Community Care Act* 1990. There are several excellent books which provide a detailed account of the history of welfare services (Means and Smith, 1998; Means et al., 2002; Means et al., 2003) but in summary the main underlying issues in welfare for older people between the 1960s and 1990s, which are reflected in Box 3.1, are:

● deinstitutionalisation with the growth of community care
● a concern about a rising tide of 'the elderly' and a downturn in the economy
● a number of scandals about older people in residential homes
● care in the community becoming care *by* the community
● ideological commitment by the government to further develop a private market in welfare services
● lack of clarity over which statutory agency held responsibility for what task
● lack of a coherent policy framework
● inflexible and traditional services not meeting the needs of older people and their carers.

Box 3.1 Policy overview, 1948–93

1942 The Beveridge Report
   Counselled against being 'lavish in old age' and recommended that pensions should be set below the subsistence level to promote thrift.

1948 National Assistance Act
   Local authorities are enabled under section 29(1) to promote the welfare of older people. Section 21 of the NAA 1948 places a duty on local authorities to 'provide residential accommodation for persons who, by reason of age, illness, disability or any other circumstances, are in need of care and attention which are not otherwise available to them'. Section 47 contains the power to remove a person from their own home in specific circumstances.

1949 Royal Commission on Population
   Noted the increasing population of older people and saw this as a threat to the nation's prosperity.

1953 Phillips Report
   Looked at the economic and financial problems involved in providing for old age.

(Continued)

Box 3.1 (Continued)

1959 Mental Health Act
Recommended care in the community; closure of Victorian asylums.

1968 Health Services and Public Health Act
Made arrangements for the provision of meals and recreation, visiting and social work services, adaptations, warden services and boarding out as well as assistance in transport to services.

1970 Chronically Sick and Disabled Persons Act 1970
Local authorities required under section 2 to assess individual need and provide services to meet the needs of disabled people.

1979 *A Happier Old Age*, DHSS
A discussion document about whether community care could keep people out of residential care, warning that 'The rise in the elderly population puts a great strain on all our pockets'.

1981 *Care in the Community* Green Paper
This document considered joint financing to promote moves out of hospital.

1981 *Growing Older* White Paper
This discussion document, produced by the Conservative Government, reinforced that care in the community must increasingly mean care by the community that is 'informal' care.

1981 *Care in Action* White Paper
Recommended strengthening neighbourhood and community support.

1981 DHSS Supplementary Benefit rules change to provide public support to residents of private and voluntary homes. This had major repercussions on the growth of private residential care.

1982 *The Rising Tide*, a Hospital Advisory Service report on the prevalence of dementia.

1983 Mental Health Act
The Act obliged authorities within resources available to promote community care for mentally ill people.

1983 'Social Services provision of care to the elderly'
The DoE Audit Inspectorate found that there was a patchy and inefficient distribution of resources across the country; it recommended home care organisers as coordinators of community care.

(Continued)

Box 3.1 (Continued)

1986 *Making a Reality of Community Care*, Audit Commission
Again ineffective service delivery and geographical inequality were
reinforced in this document.

1987 Firth Report
Against concerns that older people were entering private residential
care unnecessarily, this report focused on assessment of need.
It concluded that public support for residential care was justified.

1987 *From Home Help to Home Care*
Social Services Inspectorate Report identified. deficiencies in the
technical efficiency of home care services.

1988 Griffiths Report
Recommended Social Services to be 'enablers' rather than 'providers'.

1989 *Caring for People: Community Care in the Next Decade and
Beyond*
A White Paper advocating a wide spectrum of services to people in
their own homes, to be provided by the independent and public
sectors, but acknowledging that the bulk of care is provided by
family and friends.

1990 NHS and Community Care Act
Major legislation telling social services they would be the lead
agency in community care; introducing the purchaser–provider split
and a mixed economy of social care.

The main driver behind the Act was to curb public expenditure on
residential care after the government of the day had created a 'perverse
incentive' in relation to community care, allowing a subsidy for
entry to private residential care through the social security budget
(Phillips, 1992).

The emphasis from the Thatcher government was on efficiency,
effectiveness and economy and this was embodied in the 1990 Act.
This created the mixed economy of welfare; the purchaser–provider
split (with the local authority holding responsibility for assessment
and purchasing with other agencies fulfilling the role as providers
of service); targeting, rationing, charging for services and contracting
to the independent sector, consequently turning 'clients' into

'consumers'. These changes turned community care into a quasi-market (Le Grand and Bartlett, 1993).

The Griffiths Report (Griffiths, 1988) leading to the *NHSCCA* (HMSO, 1990b) also redressed the difficulties within the operation of social work highlighted by the Audit Commission in 1986. Through the establishment of care management, Griffiths advocated a 'needs-led' rather than a 'service-driven' approach, governed by assessment and negotiation of care packages as well as monitoring and reviewing outcomes with users and carers. Griffiths thereby identified the need for community care policy to focus on the individual user and carer.

Developments since 1990

In terms of the overall organisation of welfare services, there has been a shift towards managerialism. The *NHS and Community Care Act* (HMSO, 1990b) has been the most significant piece of legislation in recent decades. The rationale was that reorganising services along the lines of free market principles would improve economy, choice and effectiveness. Local councils in England for example, were funded for community care from a transitional grant only if they invested 85 per cent in the development of the independent sector. This was not only thought to be a device to promote choice and drive down prices through competition but also as a means to reduce the role of local councils as service providers. On this basis, the service user was seen as a consumer of services. However, there has been a robust critique of the notion of service users as active consumers, given that, for example, social workers are still required to make judgements about whether a person is eligible for services and they ultimately define what needs the person has. Older people's choices are going to be limited to what is available and affordable – if they are restricted to a limited income (i.e. do not have their own resources). Such a position led to a debate about the development of a two-tier system, that is, older people who had the financial resources to purchase resources to meet their needs (for example, a place in the care home of their choice) and those who were limited by the need to contain costs and work with those agencies that were contracted (e.g. care homes that have a negotiated and fixed weekly price for people who rely on funding for social services).

There were several problems following the 1990 legislation. Many individuals faced increased charges for social care and many carers, often older themselves, had to struggle to provide the preventative services that were necessary but now no longer a function of the local authority (shopping, cleaning). The rhetoric of empowerment and user participation was just that – there was little reality in the notion. Social workers also felt uneasy about the need for advocacy and self-determination in their practice versus resource constraint putting a lid on any effective social work practice. The quality of services, lack of funding in all sectors and the failures of interagency working were also apparent by the late 1990s.

Modernising social services

The Blair Government that came to power in 1997 has continued a managerialist agenda and extended it; its distinctive contribution being a greater emphasis on partnership, quality and continuous improvement, and evaluation and monitoring of performance (Waine and Henderson, 2003).

A raft of policy has come from central government in England, which has embraced the facets of the current government's inter-pretation and ideological commitment to regulating and improving standards. The White Paper, *Modernisation of Social Services: Promoting Independence, Improving Protection, Raising Standards* (DoH, 1998; www.doh.gov.uk/scg/wpaper) and the *NHS Plan 2000* (www.nhs.uk/nationalplan) placed emphasis on providing high quality services to public service users and ensuring that policy was more joined up and strategic, particularly regarding health and social care.

The Long-Term Care Charter set out what people could expect if they needed support from health, housing and social services. In adult services, six objectives are relevant for older people:

- to promote the independence of adults assessed as needing social care support arranged by the local authority, respecting their dignity and furthering their social and economic participation
- to enable adults assessed as needing social care support to live as safe, full and as normal a life as possible, in their own home wherever feasible

- to work with the NHS, users, carers and other agencies to avoid unnecessary admission to hospital, and inappropriate placement on leaving hospital; and to maximise their health status and thus independence of those they support
- to enable informal carers to care or continue to care for as long as they and the service user wish
- to plan, commission, purchase and monitor an adequate supply of appropriate, cost-effective and safe social care provision for those eligible for local authority support
- to identify individuals with social care needs who are eligible for public support, to assess those needs accurately and to review care packages as necessary to ensure that they continue to be appropriate and effective.

(Department of Health, 1998, p. 111)

Best Value was introduced in 1997, but was replaced with compulsory competitive tendering. Every local authority activity was subject to delivering the most effective, economic and efficient services possible and to compete with external providers. This was accompanied by Fair Access to Care which provided guidance to local authorities on eligibility criteria relating to access to services. The framework is divided into four bands: critical, substantial, moderate and low. In 2000 direct payments were extended to older people over the age of 65. This was further enhanced by the *Carers and Disabled Children Act 2000*, extending payments to carers. The payments are used to purchase services, including those from a spouse or relative to meet the assessed needs of older people.

Increasing regulation has come through the *Care Standards Act 2000* separating out the inspection of social services from the provider with the National Care Standards Commission (Commission for Social Care Inspection www.csci.org.uk) being established. Standards in relation to the workforce have been implemented through the creation of the General Social Care Council (to regulate social care workers and regulate education and training) and the Social Care Institute of Excellence (SCIE) promoting good practice in social care by reviewing knowledge to find out what works best.

A variety of further legislation has impacted on social care provision, for example, the *Carers (Recognition and Services) Act*, 1995, and the *Carers and Disabled Children Act*, 2000. These pieces of legislation provided rights for carers to assessment; the latter act followed from the Carers National Strategy which highlighted the needs of carers for information, support, care and employment (see DH website, www.doh.gov.uk). The *Disability Discrimination Act*, 1995, followed by the *Community Care (Direct Payments) Act*, 1996, and the *Health and Social Care Act* 2001 have also had implications on services for older people. The 2001 Act created Care Trusts providing integrated care along with changes in long-term care funding. The *Community Care (Delayed Discharges) Act* 2003 introduced charges on local authorities for hospital beds that are taken up by older people awaiting a social care service with the aim of reducing delayed discharges from hospital beds. This act, however, goes against the spirit of integration and partnership embodied in much of the modernisation agenda.

This strategy for modernising social care services focuses on a 'top-down' approach with the implementation of the *National Service Framework for Older People* (DoH, 2001b) as an example. The government has been active in driving the agenda for change in older people's services by identifying key goals and achievements that must be provided by health and social care agencies. These are stated in the *National Service Framework for Older People* as standards of care for all older people, wherever they live. They are standards related to the following:

1 Rooting out age discrimination.
2 Promoting person-centred care.
3 Giving older people access to intermediate care.
4 Delivering appropriate general hospital care.
5 Preventing strokes.
6 Preventing falls.
7 Accessing integrated mental health services.
8 Promoting an active healthy life in old age.

As part of the local implementation of the National Service Framework for Older People, a new role of older people's champions (a councillor and a practice development champion) was introduced to raise the profile of older people at local level (Manthorpe, 2004).

All these initiatives address the difficulties raised in *Modernising Social Services* such as the lack of effective safeguards to protect vulnerable adults from neglect and abuse; the failure of partnership;

inflexibility of provision; lack of clarity on roles and standards; inconsistency in quality and access to services and inefficiency in costs between councils. Reforms in social care have been linked to reforms in the health service (the *Health Act* 1999 together with the *Health and Social Care Acts* of 2001 and 2003 and the *Community Care (Delayed Discharges) Act* 2003) and it is in the area of health that changes will have the biggest impact on services and social work for older people in the future.

Key features of the modernisation agenda

Integrated care: multi-agency work

The importance of partnership and collaboration to provide better services has a long history but with variable outcomes; Hudson et al. comment that 'Inter-agency collaboration in the public sector has been viewed as a self-evident virtue in complex societies for several decades, yet has remained conceptually illusive and perennially difficult to achieve' (2003, p. 232). The focus on partnership, however, has replaced the competition or quasi-market approach adopted in the Thatcher years. While there is a lack of clarity about the definitions of terms such as collaboration, partnership and inter-professional working, the rationale for working effectively across agency and professional boundaries is clear (Hudson, 2000):

1 There is a demand that services are arranged to prevent the fragmentation of service delivery for service users.
2 Service users who are, by definition, often ill, worried and vulnerable should not have to work their way through complex and impenetrable systems to gain access to advice, information, support and services; service users do not fit often easily within one particular agency.
3 Charlesworth (2003) highlights the likelihood of needs being neglected when there is a lack of co-ordination across agencies and resources.
4 Finally, service users should not be the victims of boundary disputes created by poor working arrangements between agencies.

There are, therefore, a number of compelling potential advantages to multi agency or partnership working when considering the needs of service users. There are also potentially important advantages in effective multi-agency or partnerships for workers. In their study, Webb and Levin (2000) found that participants reported benefits of closer working to include a better understanding of different professional roles and closer agreement on worker responsibility and agency function. Other advantages may include the opportunity to share complex cases and associated decision-making and interventions with other workers; accessing resources and expertise from a wide range of people, and utilising and sharing one's own skill and value base in a multi-professional context, may all positively contribute to the experience of day-to-day practice. But there are also significant potential obstacles. Trevithick (2000) highlights the difficulties of working effectively across professions who use different theory and practice models and value bases. Moreover, knowledge and its relationship to the acquisition of 'professional power' can result in professionals who have traditionally been at the top of the hierarchical tree, assuming that their knowledge base and associated status take precedence over others. A team may comprise a wide range of workers but it does not necessarily follow that decision-making will inevitably be better (Trevithick, 2000). Again, a dominant professional can lead to assumptions not being challenged or being overlooked and other team members being effectively silenced. From a service user perspective, too many professionals involved in their care may, according to Finlay (2000a) be experienced as confusing, disempowering and more worryingly, have the potential for a service user to be given contradictory advice or information. Other issues have certainly impeded partnership or inter-professional working in the past, such as complex funding arrangements, protective approaches to budget holding and cost shunting, for example, around whether a service user needed a 'social' bath or a 'medical' bath (Twigg, 2000); different planning cycles and arrangements and diverse eligibility criteria. For a full discussion, see Hudson, 2000 and Øvretreit, 1997.

The aim of stronger collaboration between professionals has been recognised as a desirable development for several decades. As we saw in Box 3.1, the Audit Commission (1986) wrote a critical report of the fragmentation between health and social services and of the 'perverse incentives', for example, to admit people to care homes when other interventions might have enabled people to remain at home. The Griffiths Report (Griffiths 1988) made similar comment and recommended collaboration be imposed by linking it to financial incentive (i.e. access to social care funding). However, collaboration does not necessarily sit well with the principles of marketisation which includes primarily competition. Some strategies for collaboration were formalised, such as the requirement that local councils collaborated with health authorities and other agencies in publishing their annual community care plan which identified plans to meet the community care needs of the local community. The transitional funding for community care was given to local councils with the requirement that they invested predominantly in developing service contracts with the private and voluntary sectors. Moreover, the funding arrangements were altered for residential and nursing home care. This change meant that people could not move into a care home without an assessment of need and the requirement that social services and health trusts collaborated with each other about discharge arrangements for vulnerable people in hospital.

Partnership working is fundamental to the Labour government's agenda for the modernisation of health and social services. The *1999 Health Act* outlined the way for partnership through care trusts. The document, *Modernising Social Services* (DoH, 1998), made partnership a fundamental component of changes envisaged to create a modern and effective social care framework. The *National Service Framework for Older People* (2001b) is underpinned by the requirement that agencies develop effective partnerships with other agencies. For example, the *Single Assessment Framework* (DoH, 2001d) requires effective partnership working, and, for example, the development of trust in terms of working with the assessment findings of another assessor.

Single assessment

This strategy has derived from concern that older people's experiences of assessment have often been one of fragmentation, where a person may be over-assessed, telling their story many times to a range of professionals. This relates to a fundamentally important ideological aspiration of the government, towards effective multi-agency working and the removal of the traditional professional boundaries and associated disputes that have been dominated by the health and social care 'divide'.

The key rationale for a single assessment process includes:

- information is given once, regardless of whether the assessment and subsequent care planning or service delivery have involved many people;
- a holistic picture of older person's needs is developed which does not focus just on health and social care issues but also includes, for example, assessment of housing need and circumstance, benefits and transport;
- professionals are required to work together in trying to achieve the best interests of the older person; this also means trusting and accepting the assessment information of other workers;
- the involvement and participation of the older person are central to the assessment process;
- the depth of assessment should be proportionate to an older person's need, and four broad types of assessment are identified within the single assessment process (DoH, 2001d).

The Department of Health (2002b) highlight the importance of social work roles in a single assessment process and in terms of their ability to identify other appropriate colleagues to carry out in-depth assessments. Triggers for more in-depth assessment will usually emerge from carrying out an 'overview assessment'. Many of the other policy developments initiated by the Labour Government carry with them a requirement for partnership working. For example, the Prevention Grant, which provides resources for developing services aimed at promoting independence, has been tied to the requirement that development plans are made jointly between local councils and NHS agencies. The government has developed partnerships further by, for example, removing legislative blocks to pooled finances and lead commissioning. It is now common to see Strategic Partnership Groups working to develop strategic plans across agencies; workers traditionally employed within healthcare settings are working in teams with social workers, care managers and domiciliary care workers, and childcare teams are inte-grated with education services, and adult services are developed into Trusts. One of the crucial developments for the success of single assessment is the need to improve IT infrastructure in social care. For professional learning and development material, see www.cpa.org.uk/sap

Fair Access to Care and Eligibility Criteria (FACs)

The 1990s was characterised by increasing targeting of services to those people in greatest need. However, a lack of consistency between local councils in their provision of services to older people with similar needs led to the government introducing national eligibility criteria, Fair Access to Care FACs (DoH, 2002a) in England. Four bands describing differing levels of risk have been constructed: critical, substantial, moderate, and low (DoH, 2002a). The Department of Health guidance on setting eligibility criteria within FACs states that 'councils should prioritise needs that have immediate and longer-term critical consequences for independence ahead of needs with substantial consequences. Similarly, needs that have substantial consequences should be placed before needs with moderate consequences; and so on' (DoH, 2002a p. 5). Further information can be found on www.doh.gov.uk/scg/facs

Direct payments

Modernising Social Services also extended *The Community Care (Direct Payments) Act* 1996 enabling local authorities to make direct cash payments to disabled people over 65 (previously it had been restricted to those under the age of 65). Older people are able to opt for a direct service and/or to receive a direct cash payment, which they can use to buy equipment or care which can include that from a close family member. Although there is no minimum direct payment, the amount received is based on assessment of need, agreed between the older person and social services. The rationale is to extend choice to the user who will have greater control over their care resources. However, many older people may not wish to become employers as such and this may account for the low take-up of direct payments with only 2700 people over 65 taking advantage (Sale and Leason, 2004) up to May 2004.

Preventing dependence: intermediate care

Standard 3 in the National Service Framework introduced intermediate care at home or in a designated care setting, as a service aimed at preventing admission to hospital and enabling discharge from hospital to the community. It developed from a need to stop 'bed blocking' or delayed discharge and was framed as a problem for the health sector rather than the needs of older people. The evidence so far (SSI, 2004) finds that many intermediate care projects are achieving benefits, despite initial reservations over inadequate assessment (Cornes and Clough, 2001).

Carers

The *Carers (Recognition and Services) Act* 1995 was the first piece of legislation intended to recognise and take account of the needs and circumstances of people providing or intending to provide substantial and regular informal care to people with chronic illness and disability. Local councils are obliged to offer an assessment to carers who undertake, or are intending to undertake, substantial amounts of care on a regular basis and in any case where the cared-for person is entitled to an assessment of need under Section 47 of the *NHSCC Act* (1990). Assessment is focused on the person's ability to 'provide and continue to provide care for the relevant person' (*Carers (Recognition and Services) Act*, 1995). The local authority must take account of a carer's assessment when making its decisions regarding potential services and care arrangements (Brammer, 2003).

The *Carers and Disabled Children Act* (2000) was intended to extend the arrangements of the *Carers (Recognition and Services) Act*, 1995. A carer, providing or intending to provide regular and substantial care, has a right to request and receive an assessment even if the person they are caring for has refused an assessment of need. Local councils have discretion to provide services to support (but there are limitations to the type of help that may be provided) and help carers undertake their role based on assessment of the carer's needs (Brammer, 2003, p. 320). Taken together, both pieces of legislation represent the success of the Carers movement in highlighting the range of issues and challenges facing informal carers. Moreover, a plethora of research has provided a range of evidence on the experience of caring and the requirements of informal carers to undertake their roles (e.g. Twigg and Atkin, 1994; Dalley, 1996; Phillips et al., 2002) in the provision of care.

Anti-discrimination

Underpinning policy is the commitment to anti-discrimination. Legislation such as the *Disability Discrimination Act* (1995, s19) makes it unlawful for a person to discriminate against a disabled person. The *Human Rights Act* (1998) also highlights the rights of citizens to fair treatment, and protection by the law. The difficulties that older men and women from minority ethnic groups encounter in accessing services is well documented (e.g. Blakemore and Boneham, 1994; Chau and Yu, 2000) and legislation such as the *Race Relations (Amendment) Act* (2000) is an important legislative framework for ensuring fair treatment in assessment, as it 'places a duty on all public bodies, including local councils, to promote equality of opportunity... it must take positive steps to prevent race discrimination. In social care this duty will extend to the assessment process, planning, publishing information and provision of services' (Brammer, 2003, p. 9). This means taking an anti-discriminatory perspective throughout the care management process.

Accompanying the changes in legislation have been changes in the organisation of social services and in the social work role in the past 20 years.

The changing social work role

In the past 20 years the social work role has changed dramatically. This enables us to make sense of current practice and to understand why social workers practise as they do today. Goldberg and Connelly in their (1982) book *The Effectiveness of Social Care for the Elderly*, describe the involvement of social workers in many activities as 'assessment, in mobilising resources which range from domiciliary services to admission of residential facilities, in advocacy on their clients' behalf, in counselling and casework with both the elderly and their carers, in co-ordinating services, and in community work' (p. 85). Providing direct interventions such as counselling, as well as assessment, was central to the social work role. In the 1980s community development and the emergence of the community social worker led to the development of, for example, lunch clubs and support groups and was heralded as a way forward for working with older people as part of their community or 'patch'. But this does not point to a 'golden age' in social work provision for older people. Despite repeated attempts by successive governments, community care service was very slow to develop and a mainstay of provision for older people remained the Part III local authority residential home

(Means and Smith, 1998). While social work interventions may have included counselling and 'case work', research which examined the effectiveness of interventions found that too many cases were drifting aimlessly for long periods of time, assessments were conducted covertly and without the explicit agreement of service users, and it was difficult to define what the goals and outcomes of interventions were (e.g. Mayer and Timms, 1970; Sheldon and MacDonald, 1999). Moreover, social work with older people has long been regarded as a 'Cinderella' service and too often complex situations were left to unqualified staff (Black et al., 1983). This must have placed an unreasonable burden on unqualified staff. The Seebohm Report in 1971 led to the formation of what was termed 'generic social work' – the uniting of children's and adult services as a result of the fragmentation of services. Since then, however, specialisation has developed, mainly with qualified social workers taking on children's work and relegating services for older people to unqualified assistants. Training at the time reflected such a generic approach with the Certificate of Qualification in Social Work (CQSW) to be replaced by the Diploma in Social Work which could lead to specialised pathways, enabling people to gain more detailed knowledge and skills regarding adult services. Long-standing institutional ageism reinforced assumptions that older people's needs and circumstances were less complex or important than those of people at other points in the lifecourse. There was a pervading notion that older people needed tender, loving care and little else to sustain them through transitions which involved loss, adaptation and often fundamental change.

Most services today are organised on a specialist basis with adult service teams and sometimes teams specialising in work with older people. Since the local government reform in the 1990s, social services operate either on a county basis (e.g. Staffordshire) or from a unitary authority (e.g. Cardiff Social Services), yet, despite a top-down approach, local councils by virtue of a democratic system will have different councillors with different political persuasions and so no council is exactly alike.

Increasingly, the core functions and role of social workers in the 1970s have been stripped away and have been replaced by a managerialist approach to personal social services. This trend has developed since the marketisation (privatisation and contracting out) of welfare services by the Conservative Government in the

1980s. In the first edition of this book in 1983, no mention was made of the private sector and managerialism. The current government's approach emphasises improvement of standards through robust performance measures and a much greater emphasis on 'partnership working' (Waine and Henderson, 2003). Increasingly, social workers are engaged in care management processes (screening, assessment, care planning, monitoring and review) working with a range of other professionals who are identified as care managers. There is increasing evidence to suggest that social workers have experienced a change in their role as a result of care management (Postle, 2001). Research by Weinberg et al. (2003) found that care managers spent 64 per cent of their working week in direct and indirect user and carer-related activities and 32 per cent of their time on administration. This did not differ from pre – NHS and community care reforms. However, the content of the time spent with users and carers has shifted to a more bureaucratic assessment with an emphasis on documentation rather than counselling and supportive work. It is argued throughout this book, however, that good quality assessment must require the sorts of inter-personal skills associated with counselling skills, together with a range of other organisational and practice skills. There is evidence to suggest that social work practice is surviving in care management demonstrating advocacy, empowerment and 'skilled methods and proactive decision making' (Hardiker and Barker, 1999, p. 425) along with a serious attitude towards user engagement (Bauld et al., 2000). Lloyd (2002) argues that care management can be practised within a good social work framework if service users are kept central. On the other hand, the stress experienced by social workers in these roles as rationer has been a downside of the changes, with increased paperwork and confusion over their identity (Henwood, 1995).

Uncertainty: a key issue in social work with older people

The landscape in which social work with older people is practised has changed considerably over the past decade and will doubtless continue to change. What sorts of challenges do practitioners face in embracing these changes? Finlay (2000a) comments that 'individual practitioners face the dual challenge of holding onto their own knowledge or skill base while entering into the work of other professions, which inevitably means developing new team relationships and ways of working' (2003a, p. 105). Clearly, it is no longer acceptable to assume that it is possible to operate as a completely autonomous practitioner and this level of integration will not appear overnight. People have come from different organisational cultures and Charlesworth comments that 'where traditional roles and responsibilities become blurred, or posts are funded by different organisations, workers may question their new role. 'Which organisation do I belong to?' 'Will staff with different professional backgrounds accept my role?' (2003, p. 151). Leadership for change is crucial and experiences such as inter-agency training and professional development initiatives may provide important opportunities for practitioners to learn more about other professional roles and for developing a shared agenda. The conflict between an agency-centred agenda and a service user perspective can distort the social work role and appear to be mechanistic and bureaucratic to service users (Richards, 2000).

Social work has lived with uncertainty throughout its history and the role of social work in relation to older people has changed dramatically. One of the directions which is apparent is the shifting balance towards health than social services as lead agencies in community care functions. A key issue as we potentially face integration between health and social care and the demise of local authority social services departments is whether viewing all older people as a 'burden' and problem to be cared for will take precedence. The issue of 'bed blocking' because of lengthy assessment, unco-ordinated finance or lack of available alternative accommodation portrays older people as nuisances and social workers as incompetent, yet research evidence (Phillips and Waterson, 2002) points to the importance of timely discharge and rehabilitation as a prerequisite for preventing readmission and death. It is therefore necessary that we address this as a key issue for social work practice.

The divide between health and social care and the shifting boundaries between them has also had an impact on the funding of long-term care. Health care is free at the point of use as opposed to social care which is means-tested. The shift of long-term care from a health need to a social care need has meant a shift in responsibility for funding. The financing of long term care for older people is on the political agenda. A Royal Commission's recommendation of payment of social care services through general taxation after an assessment of need was rejected in England and Wales, but Scotland accepted and implemented this principle. The result is that in England and Wales a distinction between health and social care has to be made, often in grey areas, which cause distress for users and carers. The uncertainty of long-term funding has repercussions for older people who enter private care and find they can no longer pay their way. This is an issue social workers have to work within. A further area of uncertainty in relation to long term care is the closure of many private care homes following the *Care Standards Act*, requiring many adaptations to be made to property. This financial burden for managers, alongside the small amount they receive to provide personal care as well as meals and accommodation, is forcing many private care homes to close. Laing and Buisson (2003) estimate over 13 000 care home places in England were lost between 2002 and 2003. The financing of social care is one that extends beyond long-term care as many councils face deficits (Means et al., 2003).

Finally, an area of uncertainty in relation to social work with older people is the issue of the social care workforce in general. There is a critical shortage of social care workers working with older people. Initiatives to improve social work image are vital and the whole arena of social care, care work and domestic labour needs to have a stronger overall presentation. There are similarities between paid and unpaid care work which should be acknowledged to help us understand the concept of care in society. Work is associated with women in both spheres (a higher proportion of care workers are female compared to the workforce as a whole); both carers and careworkers are getting older with higher percentages of people aged 45 to 65 taking on paid and unpaid care work (than in previous census years); the satisfaction with work is based on 'emotional labour' (Hochschild, 1979; Gorman, 2000); the tasks are often intimate (such as bathing); many jobs are regarded as unskilled; most of the tasks are hidden and silent, and there are major issues on availability and quality of staff. The invisibility of care often gives care work a negative image. Low pay and low status underpin the problem of recruitment and retention with other jobs, for example, in retailing, attracting staff (www.ioe/tcru). Social workers are part of this larger social care workforce which faces real problems of retention and recruitment.

Some commentators (Means et al., 2002) view the reforms since the 1970s as a means of improving the organisation and costing of welfare rather than a primary focus on the quality of life of older people. Despite this, there is evidence (Bauld et al., 2000) that there are tangible benefits to older people. The Social Services Inspectorate in reviewing inspections and monitoring during 2002–3 found that there was 'strong commitment and progress in modernising services along with a fundamental cultural shift in social care to one which is focused on promoting independence' (www.doh.gov.uk/ssi/olderpeople03.htm 2004). Additionally, they noted that there was more integrated strategic planning between health and social care and integrated services at operational level, with many councils demonstrating better inclusion of service users in planning and consultation and good systems in place to safeguard vulnerable older people from abuse and poor treatment. On the downside, they also found patchy availability of information, ineffective or unresponsive referral and assessment systems and disjointed and delayed care management, superficial service-led care plans that inadequately reflected the users' needs, little support to encourage direct payments and inadequate provision to elders from ethnic minority groups. These will have to be addressed as outlined in the *Planning and Priorities Framework 2003-2006* (www.doh.gov.uk/planning2003-2006) establishing yet more detailed targets for improving services for older people. The focus here is on quality and growth of services based on the principles of person-centred care, respecting dignity and promoting choice, the promotion of independent living and a healthy and active life, and user satisfaction through timely access to high quality services that meet people's needs and partnership with carers. One of the specific targets for this period (by December 2004, all assessments of older people to begin within 48 hours of first contact with social services and to be completed within four weeks and 70 per cent within two weeks) will also place considerable pressure on social workers.

Conclusion

Part I of this book has outlined the context in which social work with older people is practised. In conclusion, we stress the need for practitioners to take a critical approach to their work, challenging the inequalities that older people face at a societal level while empowering older people at an individual level. The raft of policy and legislation has gone some way to give social workers scope to realise this. How to achieve this in terms of what skills are required and what values should underpin this leads us into Part II.

---

putting it into practice

- What are the similarities and differences between paid 'professional' care and 'informal' unpaid care to older people?
- What are the differences and similarities between the main political parties in relation to their views and policies toward older people?
- In relation to our case study in this book, Mrs Terrell, what legislation and policies may be useful in exploring her situation?

Further reading

For a full review of current Community Care legislation, refer to:

Brammer, A. (2003) *Social Work Law*. Pearson Education, Essex.

Mandelstam M. (1999) *Community Care Practice and the Law*. Jessica Kingsley, London.

Means, R., Richards, S. and Smith, R. (2003) *Community Care Policy and Practice*, 3rd edition. Palgrave Macmillan, Basingstoke.

Check out the DH website – useful for up-to-date legislation and guidance www.doh.gov.uk and Better Government for Older People: www.bgop.org.uk

part **II** | **Practice issues**

4 | Practice skills and values

Introduction: core skills and values

Chapters 1 and 2 discussed critical issues in social work with older people. This chapter considers some core skills and values required in undertaking social work with older people. Empowerment is a much-used term in all areas of social care and there is a critical debate as to its purpose and application in social work. This chapter argues that social work skills must embrace and include a commitment to facilitating the possibility of empowerment; moreover, that it is essential to challenge oppressive practice with older people. In order to facilitate empowerment possibilities, effective and skilled communication constitutes a fundamental attribute in practice. This chapter introduces key issues in communication in a social work or helping context, which are then drawn on throughout the book. Linked to communication, the chapter considers the importance of skills such as advocacy in social work with older people.

Empowerment and participation

As we saw in the previous chapters in Part I, an emphasis historically on a medical model (emphasising the biological dimensions of ageing) created the potential to emphasise dysfunction in older people (e.g. Evers, 1993). The medical model reinforced a commonly held assumption or myth that all older people would inevitably decline into ill health, disability and cognitive impairment (with the associated costs to services that such a 'burden' would impose). Second, it set in place a tendency to treat older people with disabilities and impairments as experiencing nothing more than could be expected 'at their age', that could result in those people, once again, not having access to treatments that they might benefit from. This was one root cause of age-based discrimination in health and, indeed, similar issues can be traced in the historical development of social care.

Means and Smith (1998) highlight the paucity of imaginative policy and service response to older people with chronic illness and disability, how the tendency to focus on institutional care prevailed through a considerable part of the twentieth century. Community care services were consistently slow to develop. Historically, social care services have often been provided on the basis that qualified staff are not required to be involved in assessment and intervention with older people. There has been a tendency, rather, to think about older people as an essentially homogeneous group who need 'tender loving care' and a limited range of service responses. Implicit in this response is the assumption that work with older people did not particularly require social workers to possess up-to-date theory and knowledge, demonstrated in a comprehensive skill and value base.

Other forms of discrimination have been evident in social care services. For example, financial resources allocated to care packages for older people have typically been set at a lower threshold when compared to a younger person with physical disabilities. It is the government's intention that the *National Service Framework for Older People* and national policy initiatives such as *Fair Access to Care* (DoH, 2002a) will stop discriminatory practice on the basis of chronological age.

Nevertheless, the reality is that older people may be particularly susceptible to age-based discrimination. Ageism may be experienced at individual, organisational/institutional and societal levels. At an individual level, a person may use language which is derogatory about an older person; and this includes professional people who may, for example, construct personality traits such as assertive behaviour as 'stubbornness'. On an organisational level, older people may be offered services which are inferior when compared to services provided to other people who require personal social services. On a societal level, older people do not, for example, have access to a mobility component in Attendance Allowance in the same way that a younger disabled person might have via the Disability Living Allowance.

What should be an appropriate agenda for anti-oppressive social work practice with older people? Social work practice and values should, as an underpinning principle, aim to provide appropriate and sensitive services by responding to need regardless of the social status of the person (Dominelli, 1998). Anti-oppressive practice requires practitioners to challenge traditional notions of professionalism where, for example, the 'expert' (the social worker) may exert power over the other (the older person). People in power have access to valued resources, knowledge and information. The powerful professional does the following:

- is privy to information and knowledge and they can choose when and what information and knowledge to share and with whom;
- has a notion of the 'expert', e.g. knowing more about the person than the person themselves;
- makes decisions independently and without the active involvement of the person;
- engages with procedural or administrative assessment and intervention;
- is uncreative and satisfied to use 'off the peg' solutions even if there is evidence that this may be unworkable or unsuitable;
- wants to be listened to, but neither listens nor hears;
- is unaware of the nature of structural oppressions;
- uses the language of power, e.g. jargon, technical language, insistence on written communication;
- makes little effort to make information accessible;
- solely 'calls the shots' in terms of when, how, what, how long, when the intervention and professional relationship are finished;
- behaves in a manner which communicates a belief that older people are all essentially the same.

Social workers must be able to reflect on and analyse their practice in the context of the power that they have and in conjunction with the older person's position and context (Dominelli, 1998). This emphasises an interest and commitment to process in the social work relationship together with the ability to engage in analysis of needs and circumstances with the older person. Such analysis means going beyond a tendency to assume that the location of problems inevitably rests 'with' the older person, characterised by simple labels ('depressed, demented, frail woman'). We should guard against analysis, which polarises people into particular attributes, which Brechin has identified as a form of 'essentialism' where 'social behaviour is ascribed to some particular "essence" of the individual' (2000, p. 39). Instead, a broader approach should encompass analysis of the impacts of, for example, the environment in which an older person lives; their social and emotional relationships; their access to resources; and the potential impact of lifecourse inequalities. Age or being 'old' should not be assumed to be the defining experience for a person. For example, gender, race and ethnic identity, sexual identity, professional identity, the experience of living with chronic illness, or access to economic resources may be as or more pertinent to a service user. Analysis of an older person's individual context invites us to consider, for example, the possible impact of poverty over the lifecourse and the ways that gender and age cross-cut this experience to sharpen economic inequality (e.g. Arber and Ginn, 1991).

There is much talk of empowerment in social work; indeed, it would be almost impossible to pick up a social work text book without finding significant reference to it (for a full discussion, see, for example, Braye and Preston-Shoot, 1995; Jack, 1995). Ward and Mullender (1991) have warned that empowerment and participation are such 'buzz' words that they risk becoming meaningless. Commentators such as Jack (1995) and Saleeby (1997) highlight that it is erroneous for social workers to assume that 'they' effectively 'empower' an older person. Cowger and Snively comment:

> The [social work] role is not to empower people...social workers cannot empower others...to assume a social worker can empower someone is naïve and condescending and has little basis in reality. Power is not something that social workers possess for distribution at will.
>
> (1997, p. 111)

Rather, empowerment is in the ownership of the person who seeks power or self-determination. Social workers may help to create a climate for empowerment in terms of their relationship with a service user by working together to find solutions to need, by the allocation of resources, by challenging oppressive or discriminatory practices, by providing high quality interventions that do make a difference and by supporting people to make their own choices and decisions.

Creating climates for empowerment, however, take place in agency contexts where constraints do exist and where practitioners are required to work within the policies and procedures of the agency. Eastman (1995) questions the degree to which social workers can facilitate a culture of empowerment when, for example, service users often cannot determine what is or is not provided in the context of organisational and political constraints.

He argues, however, that 'the values of respect for persons and self-determination impose a duty on workers to explain as fully as is practicable the whys and wherefores at every stage in the decision making process' (1995, p. 259). While it is true that practitioners are limited by the context of managing with finite resources, this should not be used as a 'catch all' excuse for poor practice; rather, individual practitioners should be responsible for ensuring their own good practice (e.g. Braye and Preston-Shoot, 1995) and this is likely to include being open with service users about the limitations to a service or resource or challenging injustices on behalf of an older person. Challenging injustice requires social workers to persevere and be tenacious in negotiating solutions that preserve the rights of the older person.

Communication skills

Effective communication is central to all social work practice. Forming, developing and maintaining relationships, working in situations of stress and uncertainty, assessment, planning and undertaking intervention, reviewing care, negotiating with other agencies and professionals, and many other responsibilities and activities, could not be undertaken without an awareness of the complex factors that influence communication and the ability to communicate effectively. Practitioners need to recognise and understand the complex and multiple individual, psychological, emotional, social, cultural and environmental factors that influence communication. Practitioners must engage with the complex task of recognising the factors that might influence the communication of a service user and adjust their own communication style and approaches accordingly. Consider, for example, the potential communication issues involved in the following 'typical' situations:

- an assessment of a person whose working memory is much reduced and who finds it hard to express herself when she feels under pressure;
- presenting a report based on a risk assessment to an Adult Protection case conference;
- undertaking a joint visit where a neighbour has reported a violent incident between a mother and a son who provides care and support to her;

- discussing the reasons why a person, in your opinion, cannot go home from hospital to a consultant who argues that she must have the bed today;
- working with a woman in hospital who is anxious to be discharged to die at home.

It is perhaps easy to under-estimate the skill involved in switching our communication styles and approaches to meet the demands of these diverse situations. While there may be many situations where we feel we can communicate with ease and confidence, there will be others where our confidence falters or where we feel anxious or uncertain of the demands that will be placed upon us. The situations that cause anxiety will vary from person to person. Trevithick (2000), for example, highlights the communication challenges associated for many of us when talking to people in senior positions: 'My guess is that most social workers feel more comfortable talking to service users than people in senior positions. Our own reactions can be a valuable reminder of how intimated service users feel in relation to us' (p. 53). *Developing* self-awareness through reflection, supervision and peer feedback can highlight areas of communication that might be difficult and show how we might address them.

Social workers need to approach communication with service users from a value position that each person is a unique individual. What does this mean in practice? As a first base, thinking about social work practice with older people as working 'with the elderly' can communicate a message, to oneself and to others, that older women and men are a group who are essentially all the same, rather than individual people with unique biographies, life histories and circumstances (see, for example, Bytheway, 1995). Prior to meeting a person to start an assessment, a proactive practitioner is likely to begin to think about the person and make some plans for the initial meeting. A social worker is likely to have information about the reason for referral and so may begin to ponder who else might need to be involved in the assessment process; s/he may consider what information is needed to have to hand or whether particular requirements, such as an interpreter, are indicated. These considerations constitute appropriate planning for an assessment. But, it is also essential that practitioners keep an open mind about the person and their needs. Proper preparation for a meeting is quite different from assuming that this is a 'meals on wheels assessment' or an 'admission to care'. Such an approach may serve to reinforce stereotyped assumptions and close down the possibility of creative responses to an individual person's circumstances. It not only runs the risk of dehumanising an older person, but it runs the risk too, of marginalising the real skill of social work and assessment in favour of the superficial. This kind of approach emphasises the superficial, and social work should not be about bureaucratic compliance and maintaining the status quo at all costs. Thompson (2003) has emphasised that basing assessment on discriminatory stereotypes similar to the examples cited here not only communicates discrimination but also means that the assessor will inevitably be communicating ineffectively. This creates barriers and will affect the quality and outcome of the assessment and, most importantly, the experience of assessment for the older person. Assessments, interventions or, indeed, any dialogue based on this approach to practice are likely to be evidenced by communication approaches which include maintaining control over who speaks and when; interrupting a person when they are talking; over controlling the topics of talk; false listening; making assumptions before all of the information is gathered; unhelpful questioning and inappropriate or disrespectful terms of address (see, for example, Thompson, 2003).

These approaches also communicate messages about professional power. A practitioner committed to creating environments and practices to encourage empowerment and participation must acknowledge the existence of a power imbalance and also how their practice approach can contribute to addressing those power imbalances. Assessments, in which the professional assumes control and expertise at the expense of the service user, also mean that there is a real danger that the practitioner will fail to understand the nature of a person's need; the older person may feel disempowered by not feeling listened to, respected or of interest to the assessor. This approach constitutes oppressive practice.

Kadushin (1990) helps to 'unpick' this further by examining how social workers can ask unhelpful questions in an interview or assessment situation. Leading or suggestive forms of questioning may, for example, 'encourage' a service user to agree with the social worker about the best or most appropriate route or service:

Yes, but you said you were tired, didn't you? And that perhaps a break would be a good idea, so I think you would like a little holiday at the rest home, don't you?

Too many yes/no questions are responses to 'closed' questions (those that require a limited and fixed answer such as 'yes' or 'no'). They have an important place in communication. For example, they can be very useful to verify factual information. Sometimes, they can be helpful when working with a person in extreme emotion who finds free expression impossible (e.g. Trevithick, 2000). Closed questions can also have an important place when working with people with communication difficulties. For example, a person with dementia and associated memory difficulties may find it hard to respond to some open-ended questions but can cope with a question that requires a 'yes' or 'no' response. Nevertheless, too many closed questions may communicate messages to a person that you are not interested in their story and may prevent an assessor from really understanding the nature of a need. There is a particular danger that assessment tools based on independence in activities of daily living can be presented as a list of questions by an unskilled practitioner:

Social worker: So can you get to the toilet OK?
Older person: Yes.
Social worker: Good. And um, do you, um, know when you need to, um, go?
Older person: Yes.
Social worker: So, um, you don't have 'accidents' then?
Older person: No.

Garbled or unclear questions can be difficult to overcome when, for example, emotions are running high or when an assessor is asking difficult or sensitive questions. They are unhelpful to an older person who, for example, rather than locating the fault with the practitioner, may themselves feel foolish for not being able to understand what is being asked of them. A person who is anxious to cooperate with an assessment may respond to unclear questions in a way that does not accurately reflect their situation in an attempt to 'get it right'.

So do you think the thing that's needed is to find out, um, well, establish or make clear what the situation is, um, *vis-à-vis* the difficulties you are having getting on during the day – and, um, especially with regard to getting about?

Double or multiple questions can cause confusion because a person may not always know which part of the question to respond to.

Double and multiple questions can be particularly difficult for a person with memory difficulties or someone who is experiencing considerable pain or who is perhaps worried and overwrought. It is easy to feel overwhelmed by too much information, to forget what was asked and simply feel unable to respond. As a result, the social worker can make assumptions about the person that are simply inaccurate. There is a real danger that the social worker's problems in communicating sensitively and appropriately, becomes the older person's problem!

> Where shall we meet, we can stay here, or we could go to the day room, or if you like, I could go and ask the nurse if there is a side room we could go in. What would you like?

Too many 'why' questions can feel accusatory. A person with dementia may be particularly susceptible to feeling overwhelmed by 'why' questions, if their memory is poor and the person is unable to recall the information required. The result may be that a person with dementia feels embarrassed, upset or withdrawn and, in the worse case, being inappropriately 'labelled'. Once again, the assessor's poor practice can become an older person's problem.

Social worker: Why do you think that your daughter has asked me to come and see you, do you know?
Older person: Um.
Social worker: Well, she was worried that you were trying to collect your pension when the post office was closed and everyone was in bed. Why do you think that was?
Older person: Um.

These issues can all be exacerbated by a social worker failing to observe aspects of behaviour such as signs of social discomfort or distress and made worse by the social worker 'outpacing' the person in communication, i.e. going too quickly (Killick and Allan, 2001).

The fact that it is impossible to be absolutely prescriptive about 'how' to communicate effectively highlights both the complexity of appropriate engagement and relationship building in social work and the importance of working with diversity. It is clearly important to practise these skills and to use opportunities such as supervision to discuss and reflect on communication challenges. The practice task focuses on finding communication styles and approaches that feel right for the practitioner and most importantly, meet the needs of the individual older person and the tasks at hand. As a basic foundation, the skills involved in counselling approaches are considered to be fundamentally important to relationship building, assessment and intervention (Cosis-Brown, 1998). There are a range of theoretical orientations that inform counselling approaches, but most are underpinned by the following key communication skills and values:

● non-judgmental attitude
● unconditional positive regard
● empathic understanding
● genuineness
● trust
● confidentiality
● active listening.

Assessment is concerned with working together in order to do the following:

● gather information about a person's needs and circumstances, starting with the older person's views and including other key people in the person's support network;
● identify the strengths and resources that a person has;
● examine significant changes and their bearing on current circumstances;
● seek the professional assessments of others as required for each individual person (for example, continence promotion nurse);
● analyse the needs identified and develop hypotheses as to the causes of need and potential ways to address them;
● discuss and explore the older person's views, aspirations and ideas in resolving their situation;
● plan a reasoned response with the primary aim of alleviating the difficulties experienced by the service user;
● ensure that any subsequent goals of intervention are written so that they may be evaluated after an agreed period of time.

None of these potentially complex processes could be achieved in assessment or, indeed, any other form of intervention without the ability to hear and listen. Hearing is a physiological act while listening is a cerebral act: 'just as you can look without seeing, you can hear without listening' (Kadushin, 1990, p. 244). Active listening involves the practitioner paying close attention to the service user but also communicating to her/him that they ARE being listened to (e.g. Trevithick, 2000). Communication skills, such as relevant follow-up using open questions, reflection, paraphrasing and non-verbal communication can all tell a service user that their story and the information they are giving are important and being closely attended to. Active listening is a demanding skill as it requires that practitioners focus on listening rather than allowing their minds to drift off into other thoughts; this can be a tall order for a busy social worker. It is also demanding because it requires that we achieve a balance in assessment between questions that promote active, appropriate and purposeful information gathering and listening to the person being assessed (this is discussed in more detail in Chapter 5).

Non-verbal communication may be regarded as the interpreter of verbal communication by telling us

> something about the validity of the message, its urgency, whether it is being sent humorously, seriously, sarcastically...
> It says something about the person's attitude toward the message...Non-verbal communication says something about the speaker's relationship with the listener...They help us interpret the message we are hearing...Verbal communication is concerned with 'what' we communicate; non-verbal communication is more concerned with 'how' we communicate.
>
> (Kadushin, 1990, p. 269)

(For a full discussion of non-verbal communication in an interview situation, see, Kadushin, 1990; Hargie, 1997; Thompson, 2003.) The role of non-verbal communication in interaction is fundamental to us all but thinking about non-verbal communication in respect of older people may reveal particular considerations that with forethought, planning and observation can be addressed so as to avoid the person being disadvantaged or oppressed. For example, an older person may have significant sensory impairment, which can crucially impact on their ability to participate in verbal communication on a one-to-one basis or in collective or group settings. It is important for a practitioner to be aware of these issues and also the potential solutions to them. It might simply suffice to establish if the person usually wears a hearing aid. If they do, then it makes sense, if the person appears to have difficulty hearing, to ask her/him if they need any assistance with their hearing aid. Checking whether it is fitted (correctly), in the correct ear, switched on and with a functional battery are all important. This may sound self-evident and too basic to waste words, but it is not difficult to find older people in, for example, collective care settings such as residential care where the older person struggles to fit the device and the staff on duty that morning are unfamiliar with the person's needs or have not yet provided assistance.

Older people from minority ethnic groups may need access to translation and interpreting services. There are good reasons why family members may not be best placed to offer this service, for example, family members may feel uncomfortable communicating sensitive or personal questions and information to or about a senior member of their family. Cross-gender interpreting may demand discussion of topics that are embarrassing or very sensitive if raised between men and women. It may also be difficult for a family member, with their own needs and feelings, to interpret without bias. This may be particularly pertinent for a person providing care and support to a person with complex needs when they are themselves feeling exhausted and under pressure. Under these circumstances social workers must understand these complexities and pressures and work with professional interpreters.

At other times, an older person may have communication difficulties caused by, for example, a stroke. In this context, it may be vital to work with family members or speech and language therapists in order to obtain advice and information about the most appropriate way to facilitate the older person's participation. What should never be acceptable is to *assume* that communication with the older person is 'impossible' and to rely on family members because it is quicker or avoids potentially difficult encounters with the service user. Once again, there is often a balance to be achieved between ensuring the older person is kept at the centre of the picture but also not overloading the person if they are very unwell, tired, in pain or anxious. In many situations, the person themselves can communicate their own limitations. At other times, the practitioner must rely on their practice knowledge and wisdom together with sensitive observation skills.

Eye contact is an important non-verbal behaviour in terms of its ability to communicate, for example, interest, attention, involvement and concern. Kadushin (1990) has highlighted the fact that eye contact along with all non-verbal behaviour is culturally mediated and may not be desirable when a person is communicating something which they feel is embarrassing or when their composure is threatened. Eye contact may also be avoided if the person does not want to see the reaction of the recipient of communication. These issues need to be borne in mind when talking one-to-one, especially if the talk is on issues that the person feels uncomfortable about or sensitive issues are being discussed. It is also important to consider that an older person may not have full access to the usual range of non-verbal behaviours as a result of physical or cognitive impairment. For example, a person who is blind may not 'use' eye contact as a sighted person would; a person with hemiplaegia resulting from a stroke will not have access to the usual range of hand and arm gestures that they might have; a person with chronic pain may limit their movements to reduce pain; a person with depression may appear shut down and exhibit few physical movements or, alternatively, present as anxious with rapid movements, gestures and talk.

Social workers can communicate distance or engagement by the proximity with which they sit. Like eye contact, physical proximity is culturally mediated and influenced by context, but physical distance between people is significant in any interview encounter. Thompson states that 'if we stand too far away, we will come across as, quite literally too distant' (2003, p. 126). Again, however, the individual circumstances of an older person may mean that the usual rules of proximity do not apply. A person who is in bed or who has a severe hearing impairment may require that we sit closer than might be considered usual in order to enhance hearing and participation in the conversation. A person with complex needs in dementia may need us to move more closely into their personal space in order to maximise their potential to engage and respond. These strategies have to be used with sensitivity; it would be wrong to assume, for example, that a person with dementia will necessarily feel comfortable with someone sitting inside a personal space usually reserved for people with whom they have a close or intimate relationship.

It is perhaps easy for us to under-estimate the complexity of the messages that we have to communicate to service users. Assessments, Fair Access to Care regulations, the role of different professionals, charging regulations for admission to a care home, statements of need, and care plans are aspects of work that practitioners undertake every day. But to an older person, they may all seem bewildering, frightening and off-putting. We have an obligation to try to do all we can to avoid jargon and 'speaking clearly, at moderate volume, at moderate tempo, with little hesitancy, without undue fidgeting, nervous laughter or throat clearing' (Kadushin, 1990, p. 281). This is not always easy in situations of high emotion requiring complex evaluations, information sharing and decision-making. Thompson (2003) highlights the importance of emotional intelligence in the context of inter-personal communication. First of all, social workers must be able to cope with and manage the stresses associated with working with older people who are often in difficult, stressful and upsetting situations. Second, we must be able to reflect on our own communication and the practice that goes with it. Third, we must be able to use those reflections as a means of developing and improving practice.

Finally, the issue of written communication should not be overlooked. Record keeping is an essential skill and should summarise facts, evidence, decisions, action taken, evaluation, and monitoring/ review information (Coulshed and Orme, 1998). Service users have the right to see their files and what is written about them and this right is laid out in the *Data Protection Act* (1998). There are some exceptions as to what can be shared and social workers and students on placement should be familiar with the policy of their agency. It is now commonplace for agencies to have computer systems providing, for example, information about service users, a record of involvement with the person, the input of other agencies and current care and support going to that person. Increasingly, attention and resources are being given to computerised systems that are compatible with those of other agencies and this is clearly an important component in effective partnership and multi-agency working. Social work practitioners must be familiar with the use of these systems as well as, increasingly, competent in the use of e-mail; word processing packages, use of the web and other internal monitoring and accounting systems that make use of computer software.

Care plans should be written with clarity, stating the purpose of the intervention, what will happen, by whom, and over what period of time. They should avoid jargon. Reports should be constructed to the standard required by the agency. It is important to consider the purpose of the report as this may influence the content, style and structure. For example, a report for a 'Vulnerable Adults' conference is likely to require a summary of issues identified from multi disciplinary assessment and/or investigation; evidence of risk factors; information as to the person's strengths, resources and individual context, and recommendations of appropriate courses of action or intervention. It is also good practice if the older person the report is about is aware of the contents; it should not be the case that an older person is hearing something for the first time at, for example, a case conference or a review meeting. The involvement of older people in their review meetings is discussed in more detail in Chapter 6.

Letters to service users should be written clearly and concisely. It is certainly the case that older people have been badly frightened by the quasi-legal tenor of letters about, for example, reviews of care arrangements. Actively thinking about and planning for the communication needs of a service user can prevent an older person feeling that their needs are unimportant or have been disregarded. A letter written in a small typeface, for example, may be of little use to an older person with macular degeneration. There is a legislative basis that requires us to ensure that agency procedures do not make it impossible or very difficult for a person with disabilities to make use of a service offered by that agency (*Disability Discrimination Act*, 1995, Section 21).

Negotiating skills and advocacy

A key skill in social work is negotiation. The purpose of negotiation is to reach some form of agreement, perhaps from a range of options or to resolve a disagreement, conflict or injustice (e.g. Coulshed and Orme, 1998). Thompson (2002) has highlighted negotiation skills as being essential in promoting shared decision-making and partnership. Negotiation forms an important part of direct work with older people, for example, in exploring and agreeing potential options for support and intervention. While it is essential that the older person is kept at the centre of the picture, it is also highly likely that negotiations will extend beyond the person to other key people in the system, such as:

- family and friends, including carers who may have different needs and different agendas;
- potential providers (for example, home care, day centres, voluntary agencies, residential care facility);

- other professionals and agencies involved or likely to be involved in specialist assessments, interventions and the ongoing care and support of the person;
- other departments within the organisation (for example, resource allocation panels, vulnerable adults unit, duty workers, finance departments).

This list could easily be extended but highlights the complexity of negotiating and communicating with a number of people in the system as well as keeping the older person involved in and/or informed of progress. It is possible that different people will have different views about what is needed or required and this will often make the negotiation more complex. A social worker may be planning an intervention to help a person remain in their own home; a community nurse may feel that the person should be admitted to a care home, and the home care team may argue that the hours proposed to provide support are inadequate. Negotiation brings to the foreground the importance of multi-agency working and the fact that different knowledge, skill and value bases may lead to different analyses and proposals about what is needed. This, of course, may be the basis for disagreement and conflict but can also provide opportunities for sharing expertise, learning and mutual support in complex work.

A crucial aspect of negotiation is that of 'transparent practice'. This means being open and honest in one's practice. It is appropriate to make clear to an older person what the limitations might be, in respect of care services. This means that the person has the opportunity to comment about what is offered and, indeed, have the right to complain from a position of information rather than being disappointed when raised expectations are not met. Transparency also communicates much about a practitioner's openness to work in partnership with a person rather than as the 'professional' who exercises their power by denying important information to service users. Trevithick (2000) highlights the importance of acknowledging and respecting other people's points of view – even if we hope to change their mind through negotiation. This is important when working with all parts of the system but may be particularly crucial when working with family members or agencies who may have a different view or assessment of a person's needs. The aim is to achieve a shared understanding and, to achieve this, analysis of the situation needs to be explored jointly and agreed upon (Payne, 2002). This means being able to listen carefully and in an *open* way to the concerns of the other; it is possible, for example, that the person has additional information that may change your own assessment or, conversely, that you have information about planned interventions or additional resources that the other worker was not aware of. Sharing your assessment, the evidence base for it and proposed interventions to address concerns about risk are all key ways to contribute to negotiating a shared understanding. If agreement cannot be reached, then it is important to record the difference so that everyone knows what steps have been taken in an attempt to reach agreement.

There may also be times when negotiating skills are required to achieve the best outcome for an older person and Trevithick reminds us that faced with organisational constraints, defensive practice and opposition, 'Resilience, determination and the skills of persuasion are the hallmarks of a successful negotiator' (2000, p. 145). Social work with older people regularly requires making a case at a resource allocation panel; supporting an intervention that may be unpopular with others; helping older people secure their rights and creating environments to ensure they may speak for themselves; trying to create a creative solution to a need that may be outside of people's usual experience. Many of these activities have aspects of advocacy in them. Braye and Preston Shoot suggest that advocacy 'is designed to redress power imbalances, say between purchasers and users, by facilitating discussion of options, dissent and review of the content of negotiated agreements' (1995, p. 139). But social workers are often located in the very organisations that a service user may be dissatisfied with, thus making truly independent advocacy impossible. It is important, therefore, that social work practitioners are able to assist older people to refer to an independent advocacy service.

Social workers undertaking assessment should consider their own role in advocating for older persons and also the potential need for independent advocacy and support. Older people may not have family or friends who may act as an advocate for them or family relations or the needs of the carer may mean that the person cannot act independently in the best interests of the older person. Phillipson has stated: 'advocacy is important because of the likelihood of older people entering situations where their frailties may be exposed or enhanced. This may happen as older people move into residential care, or are discharged from hospital, or embark on long-term domiciliary support' (2002, p. 62). Advocacy may be essential in terms of ensuring that an older person is not discriminated against on the grounds of their age, gender, class, occupational status, sexual identity and ethnic membership (see Chapters 2 and 3).

Advocacy has a common aim to promote the views of the individual service user either by their own participation (self-advocacy) or by being represented by an independent advocate (citizen advocacy) (for a full review, see, for example, Dunning, 1998). Citizen advocacy schemes involve an independent advocate working with a person to secure access to resources, information or services relevant to their need. There are some examples of citizen advocacy schemes developed with older persons who are particularly vulnerable to being marginalized and socially excluded (Beth Johnson Foundation, 2000). Self advocacy or user-led advocacy highlights the importance of service users being actively involved in defining their own needs and actively participating in the negotiations about how those needs might be met or addressed (Coulshed and Orme, 1998). Older people have often been without a voice in expressing choice and preference in the way their needs are met. Breaking down professional barriers and creating practice environments where self-advocacy can develop is crucial (e.g. Braye and Preston-Shoot, 1995). Sometimes, people may engage with group advocacy when they share experiences or roles in common (Coulshed and Orme, 1998). For example, a Carers Forum may provide important opportunities to ensure that carers' needs and issues are included in strategic and operational planning. Social workers may be involved in group advocacy projects with older people in other settings, for example, day care or residential care facilities. Linked to advocacy is the issue of participation and consultation in the development of services for older citizens. Øvretreit (1997) has highlighted the potentially wide continuum of involvement from giving people information about what is going to happen to them, through to service users having responsibility for deciding on and developing services.

At an individual level, user involvement and empowerment can be promoted by recognising the importance of, for example, transparent practice, negotiated solutions, providing information, and enabling older people to have the financial means to purchase their own care if they so wish. Older people have often been excluded from wider consultations and participation, which focuses on the development of services overall. Coulshed and Orme (1998, p. 63) make the point that developing effective models of involvement is time-consuming and complex organisational responses may be to adopt procedural models of consultation such as open days, satisfaction surveys and attendance on committees. Once again though, older people may be particularly susceptible to being excluded from these processes especially if, for example, they have mobility difficulties, cannot use public transport, have particular communication requirements or live in a residential care facility. If only a limited number of people can, for example, attend committees, it begs the question as to how representative their views may be of other people and especially, older people with multiple and complex needs (Brown, 2000). Creating opportunities for meaningful involvement requires organisational and cultural change and a move away from traditional, bureaucratic models of service planning and delivery towards structures at all levels of the organisation, which are geared towards creating empowering cultures.

Skills in multi-agency work

Social workers now work in even more diverse settings with a range of practitioners from other disciplines and backgrounds, for example in primary health care, hospitals, acute health and long-term care settings as well as drug agencies. Social workers bring vital practice skills and value to a multi-agency team committed to addressing the holistic needs of older people. Clarity in the knowledge and skills that social workers bring to a multi-agency intervention is important, alongside an openness to develop understanding of and trust in the expertise and skill that other professionals bring to the care and support of older people. Multi-agency working implies a willingness to share skill and expertise and to develop relationships of trust where it is possible to share work without being threatened and, importantly, to debate and discuss differences of opinion. This means that social work practitioners must develop skills in advocacy, negotiation and presentation of evidence in order to contribute to the resolution of dilemmas and disagreements. Confident participation in a multi-agency setting should mean that social workers' contributions to assessment and proposed interventions should be grounded in theoretical frameworks and take account of the evidence base that informs practice.

This chapter has addressed the basic skills required when working with older people. To practise effectively, these skills have to be underpinned by a value base embodying, among others, dignity and value of the individual. Good communication skills are needed to convey this value base appropriately, particularly during times of assessment. It is the process of assessment to which we now turn in Chapter 5.

putting it into practice

Activity 1

What does the National Service Framework set out to achieve with respect to age-based discrimination? Can you identify any changes in your agency that set out to remove discriminatory practice based on age?

Activity 2

What sorts of communication skills would be important if you were undertaking an assessment of need with Mrs Terrell? (Chapters 5 and 6).

Activity 3

What resources are in place in your agency to ensure that older people from minority ethnic groups receive an equal and culturally appropriate service? Can you identify any gaps in current practice and provision?

Further reading

Killick, J. and Allan, K. (2001) *Communication and the Care of People with Dementia.* Open University Press, Buckingham.

Pugh, R. (1996) *Effective Language in Health and Social Work.* Singular Publishing, London.

Thompson, N. (2003) *Communication and Language: A Handbook of Theory and Practice.* Palgrave, Basingstoke.

5 | Assessment

Introduction

Interviewing in social work has been described by Kadushin as a 'pre-eminently important activity' (1990, p. xi) and in the context of social work with older people, assessments of need constitute a key activity. Within the community care framework, assessment is part and parcel of a care management approach. Screening, assessment, care planning, implementation and then monitoring and review, are all components of this process (Figure 5.1).

Coulshed and Orme define assessment as 'an ongoing process, in which the client participates, whose purpose is to understand people in relation to their environment; it is a basis for planning what needs to be done to maintain, improve or bring about change in the person, the environment or both' (1998, p. 21). Developing an understanding of the needs and circumstances of an individual older person requires a practitioner to undertake an assessment to be able to gather, organise, and analyse information from a potentially complex range of sources, about an often, equally complex range of factors, such as:

- the older person's understanding and perception of their current needs and problems; what the person's priorities are; the issues and areas of need that are of most importance to the older person;
- input of other professional assessments;
- understanding and perception of other key people in the older person's network, for example, family, friends, existing formal help;
- structural factors, for example, ethnic identity and membership, gender, culture, class;

- biographical factors, for example, personal identity; approaches to problem solving, health and illness history, information about coping strategies; assessment of continuities and changes in the person's life;
- current strengths and resources, for example, individual strengths and abilities; availability of additional resources such as support networks;
- environmental factors, for example, the ways in which the built environment may impact on an older person's needs;
- risk factors.

Throughout this chapter the importance of multi-disciplinary assessment as a key to good assessment practice is highlighted. The DOH/SSI (1991) in the practitioners guide to community care identified that assessment of need should include the features shown in Figure 5.2.

This chapter focuses on the key practice issues involved in undertaking assessment with older people. First, the key principles and practice skills necessary to undertake an assessment of need are explored. Second, different types of assessment and special situations in which assessment may be complex, for example with people with dementia or who are at 'risk' are examined. Finally, key issues in good practice in assessment with older people are highlighted.

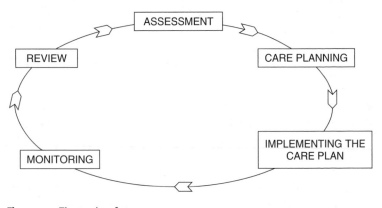

Figure 5.1 The cycle of care
Source: MacDonald (1999)

Assessment domain	May include
Personal characteristics	For example: ❑ Mood ❑ Engagement with others ❑ Personality
Attitude to self and others	For example: ❑ Views about current situation ❑ Coping skills and abilities ❑ Coping with current transitions
Health	For example: ❑ Changes in health and well-being ❑ Recent admission to hospital ❑ Treatment and medication
Functioning	For example: ❑ Mobility ❑ Washing and dressing ❑ Continence ❑ Cooking, shopping, laundry
Environment	For example: ❑ Housing ❑ Community ❑ Transport
Finances	For example: ❑ Benefits received ❑ Benefit check required? ❑ Areas of financial need indicated
Recreation and activities	For example: ❑ Long-standing hobbies and interests ❑ Changes in hobbies and interests ❑ Aspirations

(Continued)

Figure 5.2 The ingredients of assessment

Assessment domain (Continued)	May include (Continued)
Race and culture	For example: ❑ Cultural and ethnic heritage of the person ❑ Requirements regarding spiritual/religious observance ❑ Other requirements (e.g. diet, personal care) ❑ Interpreting services
Family	For example: ❑ Significant change in family system (e.g. bereavement, moves) ❑ Quality of relationships ❑ Family members acting as informal carers ❑ Key and significant members ❑ Evidence of abusive or dangerous relationships
Community relationships	For example: ❑ Friendships ❑ Social connections ❑ Community roles and responsibilities
Support networks	For example: ❑ Who the person relies on for different types of support ❑ Adequate support networks ❑ Changes in support networks
Risk	For example: ❑ The presence of danger that may lead to risk ❑ Are there relationships in the person's life that may put the person at risk? ❑ Particular vulnerabilities ❑ Strengths and resources ❑ Awareness of risk or risk potential ❑ Structural factors that may cause or reinforce risk

Figure 5.2 (Continued)

Key principles in assessment

Several key principles underpin assessment. Assessment should:

- be needs-led
- reflect individual differences such as class, race, gender
- be holistic and comprehensive
- come from a strengths perspective
- be interdisciplinary
- be participatory and empowering
- be systematic reliable and valid.

Practice skills in assessment

The practice skills required to undertake assessment create a range of opportunities, dilemmas and constraints. For example, how should a practitioner work in partnership with service users to create responsive and flexible support services in the context of a resource-constrained environment? How should practitioners manage the dilemma of espousing older person's rights to personal autonomy against a backdrop of deteriorating health and potentially increasing risk (Stevenson, 2001)? How can assessments provide comprehensive analysis of need, utilising the diverse knowledge, skills and values of other practitioners as well as the service user? How realistic is the aspiration of creative, needs-led assessment and service response in the context of managing finite resources? To what extent may current performance management initiatives impact on practice in terms of diverting practitioners and resources away from core activities towards the achievement of other outcome criteria (Waine and Henderson, 2003)?

Establishing relationships

The need to form and establish effective working relationships is crucial to social work. In an assessment context, practitioners need to be able to form relationships with a range of people often in difficult, uncertain or changeful circumstances (e.g. Phillips and Waterson, 2002). A personal network diagram (Figure 5.3) may be helpful in thinking of the connections that are potentially important to older people.

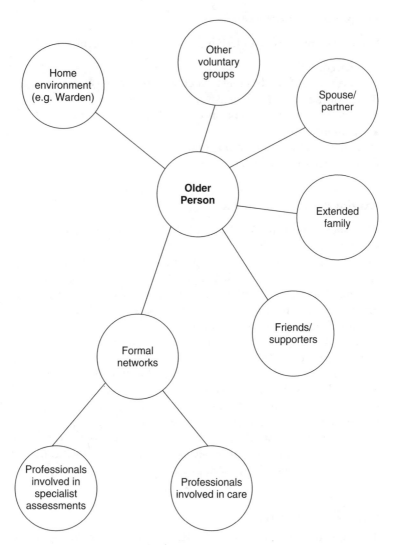

Figure 5.3 Personal network diagram

For any interview to be successful, a rapport must be established and is likely to include these elements:

● meeting each other and making proper introductions
● revisiting and clarifying the reason for the meeting

- ensuring the best possible environment for effective communication
- start where the older person is
- avoid making assumptions about what is going to happen in this meeting.

It is often the case that an older person has not self-referred but instead has been referred by members of their family or workers involved in the older person's care and support. While an older person may, in principle, be agreeable to a visit from a social worker, this does not mean that they would necessarily feel confident in their understanding of what they might expect from a social worker or assessment, the role a social worker performs, the ways they link with other professionals that may be involved in their lives and how they might be helpful. It is entirely feasible for older people to be influenced by stereotypes of social workers conveyed through, for example, the media or information gleaned from other people. An older person may be painfully aware of the difficulties they are experiencing and fear that a social worker has come with the intention of admitting him/her to a care home.

Partnership working should permeate the whole of our involvement with an older person requesting assessment or needing help and support. This means starting with some rather basic and obvious aspects of behaviour and how we present to a service user. We have to consider the importance, for example, of being punctual. Kadushin has stated:

> Lateness is an expression of the difference in status between the participants of the interview. More often the low status person is kept waiting by the higher status person...Waiting suggests to the person who is kept waiting that the person for whom she is waiting has something more important to do.
>
> (1990, p. 270)

Social work practitioners are invariably very busy, but consider what it might communicate to an older service user if you are perpetually late?

It is essential that an older person knows who you are and what you are there for. The first meeting is crucial in enabling an older person to understand your role and for you both to make introductions (e.g. Trevithick, 2000). There is research evidence which confirms that older people, in the midst of a crisis, and potentially unfamiliar with welfare services, will be unclear about the nature, purpose and outcome of assessment (e.g. Seden, 1999). Using jargon, something which often defines our professional identity or work base is an obvious obstacle to effective interviewing and assessment. This is not only because it may make the service user feel foolish (if the person doesn't understand what you are talking about), but also serves to reinforce the distance and power differential between service user and social worker. Coulshed and Orme state:

> [To] a professional worker, the term 'assessment' may be a clear and well-established concept, whereas, to others, it may come across as a vague and indeterminate term that is only fairly loosely grasped, if at all…a term like assessment can therefore, generate a great deal of mystique and suspicion if we are not sensitive to the differences between jargon and everyday speech.
>
> (1998, p. 128)

It is worth pondering how practitioners might communicate to service users; what an assessment is; why an assessment is undertaken; how an assessment is undertaken, and what the outcome might be.

It is important to start by asking what an older person's concerns are, rather than assuming that, as an assessor in receipt of a referral, you will know what the older person's concerns are likely to be. Moreover, older people may have lifelong or long-standing continuities that they wish to both highlight and preserve. A life-course approach can illustrate the way in which continuities are used to construct current identities and explain the ways in which individual older people employ strategies for managing change (Ray, 2000a).

Contact from social services might be triggered by a sudden change in circumstances; significant and long-standing continuities in life may have been disrupted, for example, an older person might have had a fall resulting in a loss of mobility and associated skills and abilities or the person on whom they relied has been taken ill or died. The person may feel frightened and uncertain about their future. They may feel overwhelmed by loss. On a practical level, basic needs may be unmet and urgent support is needed to sustain the person.

Often, social services become involved in assessing an older person as a result of their health or other aspects of their life changing over time. Assessment in this context might involve examining current care arrangements and exploring ways to adapt and amend care arrangements to continue to meet needs. The person may wish to discuss ways to maintain important continuities, or to acknowledge the losses they may have incurred as a result of illness.

It is possible that an older person may be uncertain as to the reasons for contact from social services. A person with cognitive impairment may be unable to recall a conversation with the community nurse about a visit from a social worker and may feel defensive and upset by a perceived intrusion into their lives. It is entirely possible that a referral has been made without proper consultation or discussion with an older person, who may feel resentful or worried by the contact. *The Carers and Disabled Children Act* (2000) makes provision for a carer to have an assessment in their own right. An older person in this context may feel worried or frightened that their care arrangements are at risk or that they have become a burden.

It is also likely that family, friends or other supporters may be present at a visit. It is, of course, a right for an older person to be supported by whomever they choose, and it can provide the assessor with more information about the nature of the person's support system. Nevertheless, the interviewee or assessor needs to be aware of the potential for the supporting person/people to influence the meeting:

● Supporters of the older person may have their own pressing needs or agendas.
● Confidentiality; topics may be sensitive to the older person or s/he may not wish to discuss certain issues in front of the other person.
● A concerned friend or supporter may try to 'speak for' the older person; this may be particularly acute when the person has communication difficulties or memory impairment.
● One family member's views may not represent other family member's views and certainly not the older person's view.

Clearly, undertaking an assessment with other family members or friends present may be beneficial and helpful to the older person and to the assessor. However, it is essential that consideration is given to the management of these potential issues and highlights the skill required in undertaking assessment in situations which can be tense.

Environments

Assessments may take place in a variety of environments which will undoubtedly influence the experience and process of assessment for both the older person and the assessor. For example, a person being assessed at home may have 'staying put' at the forefront of their mind, whereas a person assessed in hospital may have 'getting out' as their key goal. An older person assessed in their own home may feel more comfortable in an environment with which they are likely to be familiar. The person's home can say much about their biography and identity and this may be a sound basis for developing a positive and purposeful relationship. It also serves as an important and visible reminder to practitioners of the uniqueness of this individual person. On the other hand, the person's environment may mask difficulties; for example, a person with visual impairment may be able to walk around with confidence in the familiar surroundings of their own home but be very disoriented and uncertain elsewhere.

Observation of the person's environment and their relationship to it is immediately possible when assessment is undertaken at home. However, there are also potential pitfalls to assessment at home. While observation may give important clues about the condition of a person's home, it is important that assumptions are not made too quickly; quick assumptions can easily be nothing more than inappropriate judgements. For example, are peeling paint and overflowing gutters evidence of an inability to manage the upkeep of the house as a result of illness and disability or evidence of a lack of financial resources required to complete such refurbishment? or are they evidence of losses and changes to the person's usual support network, or not knowing who to approach to undertake the work, or a long-standing disinclination or lack of importance attached to keeping the house in pristine condition, or lack of priority in the context of managing other more pressing or important aspects of life?

Clearly, analysing the reasons for circumstances is an essential component of assessment alongside a reflective and active awareness of our own agenda. An unthinking acceptance of our own 'standards' may lead to judgmental or oppressive practice. A practitioner may, for example, consider a person's home to be 'spotless' or clean, but if the older person has always invested care and attention in her home, or if home making has constituted a significant part of the person's identity, the fact that it is no longer possible to vacuum and dust every day may be a cause of considerable worry. Indeed, it may lead to the older person assessing their home as 'not clean'.

Another common environment for an older person to be assessed in is hospital. This presents particular issues for the older person and for the assessor. Kadushin highlights the ways in which the status of a professional person may be reinforced in a hospital setting:

> The interviewee is lying down, the interviewer sitting or standing beside her. This accentuates status difference as does the difference between the sick and the well. The interviewer is dressed in street clothes, the interviewee in night clothes... The interviewee is immobilized while the interviewer is mobile which once again puts the interviewee at a disadvantage.
>
> (1990, p. 113)

It is perhaps all too easy for busy practitioners to forget that older people in hospital have lives outside of being a 'patient'. There is a danger of assessing older people as if they came into existence when they enter the practitioner's personal field of vision (Ray, 2000a). This means focusing, for example, on how an older person presents in the 'here and now'. An older person with memory difficulties may be disoriented and uncertain in a hospital environment, but can we be sure that the same disorientation and uncertainty would persist in their home environment? This is reinforced by the fact that the person is detached from the familiar things that they might usually have at their disposal (e.g. personal possessions, familiar environment). An older person may feel disempowered and vulnerable in this situation.

There are many factors that may have to be considered in the context of assessing a person in hospital, for example, the person may be worried or frightened about their future. This may be particularly critical if a member of their 'care team' has suggested that their needs might be best met by moving into a care home. People in hospital may also be concerned and worried about people they have left at home; this can be particularly relevant for older spouses who provide care and support to their disabled or ill partners. Of course, people in hospital may be fearful and worried by the diagnostic procedures and treatments they are receiving. On top of that, older people may feel stressed and distressed by being in an environment that they are not familiar with and do not know their way around. Social work practitioners can do much to reassure older persons experiencing these worries by, for example, sensitively acknowledging them and by their behaviour towards the older person, communicating respect, interest and a commitment to helping the person to express their own needs, concerns and worries.

There are other factors that have to be considered. Wards are often busy, open plan spaces where achieving a degree of privacy is problematic. Assessors need to consider how they can help to create some privacy by, for example, making use of visiting rooms or side offices or considering when they visit the ward. As well as issues of privacy and confidentiality, considering environmental factors can be crucial too in terms of promoting the best opportunities for effective communication if the older person has a hearing impairment, memory difficulties or multiple sensory difficulties. It can be almost impossible for a person with significant hearing impairment who also has to contend with background noise and activity to participate meaningfully in their own assessment.

A further difficulty relates to the issue of assessing need when a person is removed from their own environment. It may be the opinion of the multi-disciplinary team that an older person cannot move safely in the ward or get to the toilet independently. But it is possible that an older person is effectively disadvantaged by difficulties in coping with the hospital environment. Corridors are wide and long; toilets may not be close at hand, they may be poorly signposted; people may be moving past an older person at speed, the older person is likely to be feeling unwell. Home visits may be encouraged whenever possible as part of the discharge planning process and this may go some way towards enabling an older person to consider how they will manage in their home context. This also provides an opportunity for people such as occupational therapists to assess the built environment first hand and to consider ways in which the environment may be adapted to facilitate the older person's functioning in their own home.

Some of the issues raised in this discussion are also likely to be relevant when assessing older people in collective care settings. Social workers may be required to re-assess older people living in a care home if, for example, their care needs are considered to have exceeded the level of care they are presently funded to receive.

Accessing personal space for a private one-to-one discussion may, in principle, be easier to achieve as it is more likely that the person has their own room or access to a meeting room. However, in practice, it might be more complex to achieve if the person needs considerable assistance with mobility and there is an absence of staff to help. Consideration of the best time to visit is clearly important and some preparatory work about where a meeting could take place might save time and, most importantly, reduce stress for the older person. It is essential for social workers to actively consider and incorporate into their practice the social location of older people both prior to and during assessment (Thompson, 2003).

Types and levels of assessment: issues in professional decision-making and discretion

So far, we have talked about assessment in rather general terms but have alluded to the notion that assessment may take on different degrees of depth and complexity. We need to be clear about the stated purpose of an assessment and develop skills in determining what areas need to be covered and what sorts of information is collected and analysed (Kadushin, 1990) Coulshed and Orme have stated that frequently "learners attempt to find out everything in a 'scatter-gun' method: they hope to find out something worthwhile by asking more and more questions resulting in confusion from an information overload" (1998, p. 26). It is understandable that practitioners less familiar with assessment may, in their anxiety about leaving something out, 'over'-assess. But there is, as Kadushin points out, 'a fine line between interest and curiosity... The focus of legitimate interest is selective and discriminating' (1990, p. 45).

Responding to a referral for temporary help with meals

Mr Jones had fallen on his way to the local shops and broken his shoulder and arm. He was likely to be in plaster for six weeks and would require physiotherapy. Having been entirely independent he is faced with a significant but temporary, disruption to his usual activities. His daughter made a referral for help with some meals on the days when she was at work and could not help. The referral stated that other aspects of care and support had been arranged within a supportive family and church network.

(Continued)

(Continued)

Steve, a student social worker, undertook an assessment of need and was accompanied by his practice teacher who was observing his practice. Steve, discussed the purpose of assessment with Mr Jones and explained why he wanted to ask him about his current situation. Mr Jones was perfectly agreeable and again reiterated that he had luckily got everything sorted out, except dinners on Tuesdays, Thursdays and Fridays.

Using the assessment paperwork and his own line of questioning, Steve proceeded to undertake a comprehensive assessment of need which included asking questions about Mr Jones's relationship with his daughter, how he felt his memory was, whether he wore a hearing aid and whether he wanted to be referred to the chiropodist. Mr Jones responding patiently but with increasing perplexity about the range of questions he was being asked. Eventually, he commented that he 'only wanted help with dinner a couple of days a week'.

In discussion with his practice teacher, Steve acknowledged that he had 'over' assessed Mr Jones and this was caused partly by not knowing where 'on the paperwork' to stop asking questions and he was afraid that he might be told he had not 'completed the paperwork properly'. Second, he expressed concern that he might miss something crucial and this made it hard for him to know when to stop.

The potential impact for Mr Jones was feeling that he was not believed or that his own assessment of his situation was somehow inadequate. In short, Steve's approach, while well motivated, could have been experienced as oppressive. But, of course, it is entirely possible that a referral may appear to be straightforward and, in an assessment, turn out to be more complex than was first thought. Social workers must be able to encourage a person to identify their own concerns and needs as well as orientating discussion to potentially relevant areas and to being sensitively open to other areas of need emerging that might not have been initially anticipated. This involves actively listening to what the older person is saying rather than making assumptions about their likely needs and rapidly identifying service solutions available to meet those needs.

In Mr Jones's case, for example, it seems reasonable to ask him about current support arrangements. Supposing in Mr Jones's account, he had omitted to say anything about going to bed and getting up, it would be reasonable to ask how this was being tackled. Moreover, an assessor might be concerned about how Mr Jones was going to manage the steep stairs up to the bathroom and bedroom. It would be sound practice to ask Mr Jones how he was tackling the stairs in order to go to bed and get to the bathroom. On the basis that Mr Jones was emphatic about his total independence prior to his accident, it would be harder to justify asking about his memory span or undertaking some form of 'mini mental' test in assessment – unless of course, you became concerned in the context of the meeting that Mr Jones did appear to suffer from memory or other cognitive difficulties.

At the other end of this continuum is the potential to under-assess. That is, to fail to assess to an appropriate breadth or depth and, thus, miss important areas of need or concern for the older person (the aim of 'overview' assessments in Single Assessment Frameworks). There may be a number of reasons for a practitioner failing to assess to an appropriate breadth or depth, for example:

● focusing on procedural assessment (i.e. checking eligibility for a service) and failing to 'hear' the older person's needs, issues and concerns;

● making assumptions about what is needed before undertaking an appropriate assessment. This approach may again be driven by service solution approaches.

● practising within assumptions informed by stereotypes. Assuming that because someone is old, they will behave in a particular way, need a particular range of services or respond in a particular way is likely to create the potential to make decisions far too early in the assessment. Kadushin states:

> A worker can fall into the trap of tending to listen to those things which confirm the assessments made early and failing to listen to communications which contradict the conclusion he has come to...The stronger, more persistent, more inflexible, the stereotype a worker brings to the interview, the more certain he is that he knows what the interviewee will say, the less inclined he will be to actively and flexibly listen.
>
> (1990, pp. 250–1)

● failing to consider the importance of theoretical frameworks to inform assessment practice.

While, increasingly, assessments are formalised in the context of pre-defined assessment tools, we would argue that good assessment practice is not about proceeding through the assessment framework in a step-by-step fashion. Stevenson has highlighted the potential danger of a 'procedural preoccupation...where the danger is that these mechanisms become dominant and impair the face-to-face relationships' (1996, p. 207). But assessments should neither be unsystematic nor unfocused chats (Thompson, 2002) and nor should practitioners have a lack of detailed knowledge and under-standing of the content of the assessment format, its theoretical basis and its desired outcomes. Rather, we wish to stress the skills involved in using assessment frameworks in a way that emphasises:

● the uniqueness of each individual;
● the ability to work in partnership with individuals in an anti-discriminatory way;
● the ability to make complex decisions about the depth and range of assessment;
● the skills involved in analysing need, risk and aspiration;
● the ability to pull these factors together to move towards providing services, information or support.

An over-focus on 'the forms' may locate the expertise in a questioning model of assessment or a procedural model of assessment with the practitioner. Smale et al. argue that while a questioning model of assessment

> may identify basic needs, it does not address the fundamental goals of increasing choice, maintaining independence and maximising people's potential. Additional skills are needed for work with people that empowers them to have as much control over their lives as possible, and specifically enables them to exercise choice in how their needs are met.
> (2000, pp. 133–4)

In contrast, the 'exchange model' is based on a partnership approach and starts with the premise that the individual person will have views about their own situation and needs. The process of defining, analysing and agreeing individual needs and priorities is a negotiated act between the older person, the assessor/s and others in the older person's system (Smale et al., 1993, 2000). An exchange model carries with it the importance of encouraging service users to identify the strengths, abilities and coping strategies that they bring to a situation of change and challenge (Saleeby, 1997). Conversely, an approach to assessment which is deficit-oriented is likely to reinforce stereotyping tendencies and to promote and communicate the notion that an older person is not entirely capable of making their own decisions (Kadushin, 1990).

Several tools exist which can assist in aiding an assessment and in collecting information in a participatory manner. For example, a personal network diagram (Figure 5.3) provides a visual and participative way of describing a person's social network. Figure 5.4 describes the network of an older man who was responsible for caring for his son who had enduring mental illness.

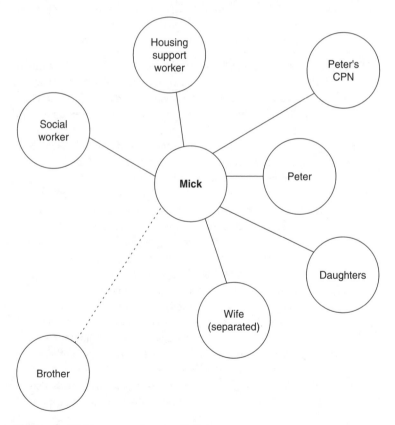

Figure 5.4 Mick's personal network diagram

Assessment in complex situations

Older people with dementia

This chapter has highlighted the importance of keeping an open mind about all assessments. A number of fundamental practice issues are raised when assessing and/or planning and undertaking interventions with persons with dementia. For example, when is it appropriate to intervene in the life of a person with dementia? How should practice be informed by a person's ability to make informed decisions about their care, and how should judgements be made about the person's ability to make informed decisions? How much risk is acceptable in the life of a person with dementia? Consider the practice issues that are raised in this referral received into the social work team at a community hospital in Scotland:

Mrs Terrell is a widow, aged 85. Although originally from the Western Isles, she now lives in a small villa in a small industrial seaside village. She and her husband met during the war when he was stationed in the Western Isles. They bought the villa when he was working as a nurse at the local cottage hospital. When she was 45, Mrs Terrell took a job doing a night shift as an auxiliary nurse in the same hospital. She worked there until she was 60. Mr Terrell died four years ago. Mrs Terrell has probably had dementia for many years but it became much more of a problem when her husband died. Her coping ability varies greatly from day to day. Some days she stays in bed and often wets it. Her personal hygiene is not very good. She leads a very quiet life and may be depressed, having been a sociable woman much involved in the local Free Church, which has now closed and the congregation attend the church in Seaport. Mrs Terrell is a Gaelic speaker and is struggling to remember her English. Neither of her daughters speak Gaelic.

Mrs Terrell has a daughter (Jane, aged 58) in Toronto who is a head teacher and married without children. She comes over to visit every summer and is getting more and more insistent that her mother cannot remain at home any longer. She is deeply offended by her mother's personal hygiene and has lots of arguments with the social worker about what should be done. She insists her mother is 'at risk'. Mrs Terrell also has a daughter (Heather, aged 60) who lives in the local city of Seaport.

(Continued)

(*Continued*)

Heather has five children and eight grandchildren and manages to combine being a dinner lady, a frequent childminder of her grandchildren and twice-weekly visits to her mother for whom she shops and cleans.

Mrs Terrell is in poor health physically since she has late onset diabetes, which was diagcnosed a couple of years ago. She had never understood the implications of this for her diet. She also has a heart condition, which necessitates water tablets as well as medication for her heart. She is not good at taking her tablets consistently. She has been tried on a cognitive enhancer but it was not successful so it was withdrawn.

Mrs Terrell was admitted to hospital via accident and emergency after being found unconscious at home by her daughter.

It is possible that increased emphasis on the tasks associated with care management may be in conflict with aspects of good practice in dementia care. For example, an emphasis on fast throughput and closure may be contra-indicated in the current evidence base in dementia care. Tibbs (2001), for example, cautions against one-off visits and repeated closure of work with a person with dementia. Brief or single visits mean that practitioners cannot hope to get to know a person and may make inappropriate judgements and assessments of need as a result. Killick and Allan state: 'we should never generalise from one particular incident; there can be marked variability in the level at which the person operates' (2001: p. 112). For example, a person with dementia may, in the afternoon, feel exhausted by the effort of coping and managing and respond very differently in the morning, after they have had the chance for a rest. But this could just as easily be reversed; a person might feel more able to cope later in the day and feel very slow and fuzzy first thing in the morning. Understanding the complexities unique to one individual takes time and usually cannot be achieved in a single visit. Adopting a holistic or 'person-centred' (Kitwood, 1997) approach to dementia care also requires practitioners to engage with their practice in a reflexive manner. For example, Killick and Allan (2001) comment on the impact of living in a 'hyper-cognitive' culture where intact memory and effective cognition are fundamental to our views of 'person'. They argue that this is reinforced by our emphasis on independence and autonomy. It is worth reflecting on our own thoughts about this; to what extent do we rely on the 'usual' forms of communication when undertaking assessment? How does it feel to us to be with someone who has a disrupted short-term memory and serious difficulties communicating with the spoken word? How easy is it for us to change our practice to adopt other strategies that rely less on spoken word and more on emotion, observation, non-verbal cues and other means of aiding communication such as visual materials?

A person with dementia, like anyone else, is likely to need time to build a relationship with a person who is unfamiliar to them. Of course, the need for time is especially important, given the challenges to memory and other areas of cognition the person with dementia is likely to be experiencing. Clearly, the development of a relationship is essential if people with dementia are to have any chance of participating meaningfully in processes such as an assessment of need and planning interventions. A consistent practitioner may provide valuable insights, information and evidence about how a person has remained stable or changed over time.

At the beginning of any assessment with a person with dementia, gaining access, particularly if the person lives alone, is crucial. Tibbs states: 'the social worker often has to draw on all her/his interpersonal skills and ability and use lateral thinking in order to gain entry to the house and access to the situation' (2001, p. 70). Imagine how a person with memory and other cognitive difficulties may feel about a visit from an unknown person or a person who is unfamiliar, and perceived as 'being in authority'. Feelings might include fear, anxiety, suspicion and embarrassment. The community social worker who arranged home care with Mrs Terrell began a relationship with her by visiting jointly with the community nurse whom Mrs Terrell had known since she was a child. This practice links with Killick and Allan's (2001) observation that enriching an encounter may provide important cues and clues to aid recollection and, most importantly, enhance the person's emotional comfort and security about the contact. The social worker talked with Mrs Terrell about who she was but also emphasised pleasure in meeting her and the importance of 'getting to know her' rather than starting the interaction with a description of an 'assessment of need'. This does NOT mean that a person with dementia should ever be lied to or treated like a child. Rather, the social worker must use their reflexive skills to build the interaction based on how things are *at the time of the interaction*, rather than relying on the prescriptive format of, for example, an assessment tool. This example highlights the importance of social and emotional contact and engagement.

Indeed, researchers have emphasised the fact that as dementia progresses, people may be less engaged with issues of task and function and more involved with their emotional life such as need for warmth, security and attachments (for a full discussion, see Kitwood, 1997).

Developing a relationship as a basis for understanding a person's strengths and needs is crucially important, especially for people with serious memory difficulties who potentially also find it harder to communicate using words. The emphasis on relationship does NOT mean that understanding and analysing needs and strengths are unimportant. Rather, it is often crucial to build a relationship BEFORE making judgements about needs, strengths, risk and danger.

Clearly, practitioners need considerable inter-personal skills and the ability to use language and communication skills with sensitivity. Many of these skills were discussed in Chapter 4. The issue of asking questions of a person with dementia raises particular issues for the person. But it also raises issues for the practitioner, faced with undertaking an assessment and likely to be a product of a long socialisation in the 'rules' of conversation and communication. From the perspective of the person with dementia, it is easy to imagine how stressful a range of 'how' 'why' and 'when' questions might be, particularly if there is the added anxiety of being 'investigated' or fear of being 'put in a home' or 'forced' to receive unwanted services. It is not until we bring to consciousness the issue of questioning that we become aware of how much our conversation is dominated by them, particularly when meeting someone for the first time. The following ideas provide some suggestions for engaging with a person with dementia but there are no absolute rules as each person's experience and journey through dementia will be unique to them. It is true to say that what works well for one person may be very unhelpful with another person; it is also the case that a person in early dementia is likely to require a different type of communication and engagement than a person in dementia with more complex needs. Reality orientation approaches for persons with complex dementia are now considered to be unhelpful. A person with significant memory impairment is likely to benefit from practitioners who avoid unnecessary questions that burden memory (Killick and Allan, 2001) For example, 'Do you remember I came last week to see you?; can you remember who I am?' Rather, 'I am Clare. We had tea together in your kitchen on Tuesday.'

Starting communication very much depends on factors such as the person's ability to cope with new situations, how they are able to concentrate on conversation, the nature of their need, how comfortable the person feels with you. But it also rests on the practitioner too. Killick and Allan (2001) draw attention to the importance of the practitioner being *prepared* to engage in communication with a person with dementia. This means planning, thinking about the encounter and not assuming that it is possible to rush into the house and proceed to do an assessment by talking 'at' the person. A good starting point could mean focusing on an aspect of biography or a compliment. For example, complimenting a person on their outfit; 'I do like the colour of your dress; it suits you.' People may be very happy to talk with you about their family and photographs are often a good source of conversation. It is possible that the person will talk about their deceased partner as if they are still alive; this can be disconcerting. A 'person-centred' philosophy asks that we start where the person with dementia starts from; this means that it is not appropriate, however sensitively approached, to remind the person that their husband/wife/partner has died. Rather, it is better to listen carefully and responsively to the person and perhaps reflect back some of the emotion or content of the conversation (for example, 'he sounds like a very special man'). Killick (1997) has highlighted the emotional pain caused by an unthinking use of 'reality orientation' whereby the person is told that their partner/parent is dead and they experience the news as a new grief. This can, of course, happen many times a day, and if a person is stuck in a perpetual state of grief, it is hard to see how they could experience well-being. It is also important this disorientation is not assumed to be a 'permanent' and 'all-encompassing' state. A person may, for example, have reflected back on the comfort that came from the lost relationship because they were disoriented or made anxious by your visit! We can doubtless all think of times when we have clung to the familiar out of anxiety or fear of the unknown. It is possible that at another time, the person will be fully aware that their partner/parent has died. Even if this were *not* the case, it would be wrong to assume that the person would be inevitably disoriented in every aspect of their lives or unable to give an opinion about their circumstances.

Other ways of beginning a conversation might focus on, for example, long-standing activities that the person has been involved with. The social worker for Mrs Terrell was able to talk with her about her knowledge of local history and her role as a church elder.

These skills constitute long-lasting memories, which were very much intact for Mrs Terrell. This was helpful not only in breaking the ice, but in validating and valuing Mrs Terrell as an individual with her own unique biography and identity.

When questions are asked, it is essential that the person is given time to answer rather than assuming that a silence is a non-response. Killick and Allan (2001) highlight how easy (and oppressive) it is to 'outpace' a person by the speed of your talk, questions, responses and even walking. A practitioner's life is often a hectic one and so it is important to consciously remember to slow down with a person with dementia, and take an evidence-based approach despite agency pressures to undertake a certain number of visits that day. The importance of active listening is highlighted in good practice in all assessment, intervention and counselling. It is vitally important in communication with a person with dementia. It may be that a person may appear to talk in a way that does not make sense. Killick (1998) highlights that actively listening (and not interrupting) leads to clues about the meaning and relevance of the communication to the person. It is often the case that biography plays an intensely important role in a person's attempts to communicate and should not be overlooked.

Joe was admitted to the assessment ward following an acute deterioration in his well-being and cognitive abilities. He had lived happily with his daughter for the past six years. During his stay on the ward, Joe spent a great deal of his time 'miming and acting out' a range of activities. He also often became agitated with other patients and tried to encourage them to 'get going' and 'move themselves'. He responded to the senior staff with politeness and attention but was often dismissive of support staff. His daughter was able to explain that Joe served in the Navy during the war and was a cook on board a submarine. It was possible to see how Joe had made sense of being in hospital by returning to this time (when perhaps he often felt frightened, out of control and unable to influence the outcome?). The ward became the submarine; the patients, ratings who were clearly not pulling their weight and the staff either senior or subordinate to Joe. His daughter confirmed that she felt his miming and acting was Joe cooking in the submarine galley. The hypothesis was confirmed when Joe refused to enter the small visiting rooms to the side of the ward; each door had a porthole window and a blue carpet!

Assessment often involves working with a much wider system than a single person. Specialist assessments are likely to be part of comprehensive assessment and families and friends are also likely to participate in an assessment process. Carers' assessments may also be undertaken. In addition, assessments are likely to be conducted in family systems. It is important to consider how assessment strategies should work to include the person with dementia (who may be marginalized by people talking for them) and also, consider the needs and circumstances of family carers and supporters. Tibbs (2001) highlights the potential dangers of overlooking family members and their role in the family system. Practitioners now have a legal duty to offer assessments to carers. Carers may feel stressed or anxious about their circumstances and must have time to talk about them. Carers may be facing very difficult situations and feel at the end of their tether. They may feel very upset by the changes in their loved one. Practitioners often need to be clear with family members about the best way to proceed with an assessment. This does not mean railroading family members into doing things 'your way' but perhaps by clear discussion and agreement, ensuring that everyone involved can participate and contribute their views, experience and opinion.

It is important that practitioners assessing people with dementia and their carers, receive appropriate training. People with dementia have distinct needs which can easily be overlooked or completely misunderstood by an untrained practitioner. Ideally, practitioners working with people with dementia should do so on a very regular basis and work in a setting where good practice can be shared and disseminated. Attention to the existing evidence base suggests too that people with dementia should have their cases kept open (Tibbs, 2001) rather than closed, so they do not need to face making a relationship usually with a completely different practitioner at some point in the future. Moreover, practitioners working in this field must be aware of the legal basis for intervention in specific aspects of the life of a person with dementia. A person with dementia may, for example, be vulnerable to financial abuse or have grave difficulties in coping with their own finances. Practitioners need to understand the criteria, process and implications for the service user in applying for legal interventions such as Appointeeship, Enduring Power of Attorney and the Court of Protection (see, for example, Brammer, 2003).

Assessing risk

There is a great deal of emphasis in current practice on risk assessment and risk management. Appropriate assessment and intervention to address risk are vitally important. However, there is a danger that the term 'at risk' can be used uncritically or on the basis of a superficial analysis of the factors that may contribute to the presence of risk. Consider, for example:

Mr Jones is at risk in his own home.
At risk. Needs 24-hour care.

Risk in these examples is a term that appears to require no explanation or critical analysis. Moreover, the notion of risk may be used as a short-hand note to indicate severity of need and thus secure access to finite resources. A consequence of this for older and vulnerable service users is that being 'at risk' becomes *the* defining label and effectively outweighs other aspects of the person's identity which might offer a wider definition of the person. Kemshall comments on the impact that images of frailty and dependency have on our social construction of ageing. 'This powerful stereotype has been used to patronize and increase the dependency of older persons, and to undermine their capacity to make choices...Choice, a central principle of community care, can be significantly undermined by professional desires to prevent risk' (2002, p. 75).

The concept of 'risk' is far from straightforward and is, in reality, a contested and relative term. Who is at risk, and why, from what and by whose assessment? Brearley (1982) defined risk in relation to the relative variation in possible outcomes and probability, providing information about the likelihood of potential outcomes occurring. Increasingly though, 'risk' is taken to mean danger (Kemshall and Pritchard, 1996) and Titterton comments, 'in the care of vulnerable people [risk] is typically taken to mean the threat to the wellbeing or welfare of the individual, their relatives and members of the public and staff alike. The concept is often interpreted as dealing with the probability of an unfortunate event occurring' (2001, p. 219). But we all take risks and they are clearly an essential part of our lives and indeed, may be seen to contribute to our quality of life (Norman, 1985b; Counsel and Care, 1993) and rights to autonomy. A more balanced view of risk including potentially positive outcomes as well as potentially negative consequences is called for.

One issue is where or how practitioners draw the line between 'acceptable and unacceptable risk' and decisions are usually focused on an analysis of whether the person is mentally capable of making an informed choice or decision (Stevenson, 2001). The draft Mental Capacity Bill (2004) is intended to provide a clear statutory framework to 'empower and protect vulnerable people who may not be able to make their own decisions'. The bill is underpinned by five key principles; perhaps the most important is a *presumption* of capacity. Set alongside this central idea are the practice-based requirements that people are supported to make their own decisions; that interventions must be based on the least restrictive options and on the basis of the best interests of the person. Lack of capacity will be assessed and it will no longer be acceptable to assume someone lacks capacity by virtue of their diagnosis. This recognises, for example, that a person with dementia is often able to make many decisions affecting their lives. Clearly, this legislation will have far-reaching consequences for assessment practice and interventions in the lives of older people for whom the ability to make decisions is identified as an issue.

The critical debate on risk highlights the potential dangers of engaging in a narrow or surface assessment of risk. For example, it is argued that the move towards managerialist practice agendas has highlighted administrative procedures and care brokerage at the expense of deeper analysis of social behaviour (Postle, 2001). Moreover, the way that risk is constructed is likely to influence the ways in which it is engaged with, resulting in narrow assessment and intervention practice. For example, an emphasis on risk and mental health might focus on assessing the risk of danger to others and danger to self. However, Tanner (1998) highlights the fact that people with mental health needs experience a greater range of risks than they actually pose. Risk assessment in respect of older people may be influenced by the social construction of ageing which emphasises the vulnerability of older people and potentially ageist views about the inevitable decline into dependency of very old people. Risk assessment on this basis might focus on 'paternalistic' interventions aimed at removing risk. Moreover, the location of risk with the individual may obscure structural oppressions and disadvantage that are fundamental to the experience of risk for an older person. An older person may be at risk of hypothermia because s/he cannot afford to pay the heating bills or at risk of loneliness and isolation because they are the last surviving member of their social and family network.

Analysis of risk also requires us to consider the fact that an older person may be at risk from the very interventions that are designed to remove risk. Pritchard (1997) highlights the real risks of living in residential care to include; abuse, injury, falling, getting lost, disorientation, isolation, immobility, ill health and death. The importance of occupational identity for persons with dementia and the negative and damaging consequences of occupational poverty in care homes have also been highlighted in research (Perrin and May, 2000). This does *not* mean that interventions should never include admission to a care home or that care home environments inevitably fail to provide good quality occupational input. Rather, the point is that assessment of risk should include a much deeper analysis, including an assessment of the potential for new risks to occur as a result of resolving the original risks.

As well as gathering information about the nature of the risk a person faces and the dangers or hazards that might promote a negative outcome, risk assessment should include consideration of the person's strengths and resources (Littlechild and Blakeney, 2001). Individual strengths and resources may provide an important basis for addressing need and risk. Risk assessment must also include evidence from other sources; family members and other professionals may have vital information to contribute to an assessment. But it is also likely that different people will have different definitions of risk and what is acceptable; indeed, their own preferences will inevitably influence their contribution to the story. There is at least a theoretical acceptance that appropriate risk taking is desirable and that a risk minimisation approach as a standard service response should be resisted (Davies, 1998). Interventions aimed at ameliorating the potentially negative outcomes of risk should be underpinned by evidence-based practice or with an awareness of where evidence does not exist or is of unsatisfactory quality. Moreover, practitioners should be supported by organisational frameworks that make clear the approach to risk taking and risk management. Interventions should focus on the least restrictive alternative and aim to meet the aspirations and goals of the individual service user rather than organisational convenience or expediency. Clearly, practitioner interventions should be informed by a sound understanding of the law Titterton states that 'legislative provision as it exists at present tends to focus on constraint and restraint and risk is largely conceived of in a negative and constraining manner' (2001, p. 228).

Social workers are likely to encounter situations where an older person is at risk because of abuse. *No Secrets* (DoH, 2000) focuses on abuse as violations of civil and/or human rights and cites categories of abuse (for example, physical, emotional, sexual, financial, neglect and harassment resulting from sexist or racist abuse). Importantly, the *No Secrets* document recognises that abuse may occur in, for example, service environments such as care homes, day care centres or other formal types of provision. The document highlights the importance of local councils, as lead agencies, to develop robust multi-agency policies and practices to protect people vulnerable to abuse. Social workers should be familiar with their agencies' policies on assessment and intervention in abusive situations and have received multi-agency-based training in this aspect of work. (For a full discussion of legal provision for particular types of abuse, see, for example, Brammer, 2003.)

There are a number of further issues concerning assessments, such as who should carry out the assessment, confidentiality issues and the content of an assessment (carers' role; breaks and social life; physical well-being and personal safety; relationship and mental well-being; care of the home; accommodation; finances; work; education and training; current practice and emotional support; wider responsibilities; future caring role; emergency/ alternative arrangements; agreed outcomes and charging). Any caregiver assessment tool therefore should be designed to collect information (primarily from the carer's perspective) on different areas of the carer's situation, to analyse areas of difficulty and strength and to assess what services might be best to meet the needs of carers.

Conclusion: key issues in good practice in assessment

This chapter has introduced readers to a range of practice issues for consideration in assessment. Clearly, assessment is a complex activity requiring effective and skilful practice. The key issue in assessment is to produce a comprehensive understanding and analysis of the needs of a service user and their immediate support network. To achieve this, a number of skills have been highlighted, including the importance of assessment in the context of an exchange model. Partnership work with service users requires that practitioners take seriously the importance of working with a person to understand their own perceptions and experience of their circumstances. Transparent practice means being open and honest in our dealings with service users, for example, pointing out differences of opinion in the assessment process may be difficult but is usually preferable to trying to gloss over them. Service users require information if they are to make informed decisions about the range of choices and options open to them; social workers are well placed to provide information and also to assist older people to access other resources and services which may assist them. We have an ethical responsibility to ensure that the process of assessment is understood along with its range of potential outcomes for the service user and their supporters. It is these outcomes which we turn to next and discuss care planning, monitoring and intervention.

putting it into practice

Activity 1

To what extent does your current assessment practice explore an older person's strengths and resources? How could you work with an older person to ensure that strengths and resources were part of your intervention/care planning?

Activity 2

What sort of preparation would you need to consider if you were planning to assess an older person who was currently staying in a care home for respite care?

Activity 3

Outline the main elements of the 'exchange' model of assessment. To what extent might this approach help to promote partnerships with older service users?

Further reading

Milner J. and O'Byrne P. (2002) *Assessment in Social Work*, 2nd edition. Palgrave, Basingstoke.

Smale, G., Tuson, G. and Statham, D. (2000) *Social Work and Social Problems; Working towards Social Inclusion and Social Change*. Palgrave, Basingstoke.

Stevenson, O. (2001) 'Old people at risk', in P. Parsloe (ed.) *Risk Assessment in Social Care and Social Work*. Jessica Kingsley, London, pp. 201–16.

6 | Care planning, monitoring and intervention

Introduction

This chapter considers how assessments of need are translated into interventions, the receipt of services and resources, and how those interventions and care/support arrangements are formulated into a written care plan. Care plans should identify the goals of intervention, how those goals will be addressed, by whom and to what purpose. As well as providing an explanation of what is being attempted to address an individual's needs, a care plan also forms the basis for reviewing and evaluating the outcomes of agreed goals; in terms of the success of the intervention and also in respect of the quality of practice that underpins it.

This chapter discusses the role and importance of care planning and begins by outlining the legislative basis for the provision of services and resources to older people. Next, the importance of care planning as a means of confirming the goals and plans of intervention is discussed. The need to ensure that care plans are linked to identified needs developed from analysis of assessment is highlighted. The importance of monitoring care arrangements and reviewing and evaluating the outcomes of intervention is considered.

Care planning and monitoring are only one part of social work. This chapter also looks at direct social work interventions such as crisis intervention, task-centred work, cognitive behavioural therapy, counselling, networking and working with carers. These have been chosen as the relevant interventions with individual older people and their support systems that are likely to be experienced by social work students and should become part of their repertoire of developing skills. The list is not exhaustive but aims to give the reader a flavour of the strengths and weaknesses and the contexts in which such interventions operate.

Underpinning this chapter is the conviction that interventions aimed at alleviating the challenges that may be experienced in later life must aim to respond to and address the diversity of older people's lives. This represents a significant challenge in practice environments which focus on providing services to meet needs considered essential for basic survival. In this context, Hughes warned of the dangers of care managers becoming 'a mechanism for the exploitative rationing of insufficient resources' (1995, p. 102). Negotiating and implementing interventions, services and resources and preparing a care plan are complex tasks which Smale et al. (1993) define as the representation of a complex set of human relationships. Planning and developing an intervention and subsequent care plan, therefore, should not simply be a matter of pulling a range of goods 'off the shelf' and applying them to the life of an older person, regardless of the person's individual biography, their needs, and what their own aspirations or preferences might be as to how those needs are addressed. Mrs Terrell's circumstances highlight a potentially complex range of needs, together with a requirement to work in a complex system populated by family members, other professionals, agencies and resources.

Planning and preparing for Mrs Terrell's discharge from hospital

Mrs Terrell has been in hospital for almost two weeks. Her health has improved as she has been receiving regular medication for her diabetes and regular meals. Mrs Terrell's well-being has also improved; her general mood is better. She is more active and enjoys helping with the meal trolley and coffee trays each day on the ward. This work is very familiar to Mrs Terrell, given her long history of working at the hospital; this has been very helpful in enabling Mrs Terrell to feel settled on the ward. Mrs Terrell's cognitive state has also improved and this is thought to be directly attributable to her diabetes being under control and receiving a regular diet.

Having reassessed Mrs Terrell, the social worker (Kate), in conjunction with other healthcare professionals and Mrs Terrell's family, has been actively planning her discharge. The social worker is leading on exploring appropriate care and support arrangements which respond to

(Continued)

(Continued)

Mrs Terrell's needs. There have been differences of opinion about the way Mrs Terrell's discharge should be planned and Kate has to actively consider and work with these differences. This has involved considerable negotiation and problem-solving.

Mrs Terrell is adamant that she wants to go home and is clear that she cannot be 'forced' to do otherwise. Although Mrs Terrell's memory is impaired, her capacity to say what she wants is clear and she retains a strong connection to her home and neighbourhood. Heather, her daughter, who is unwell, wants 'what's best' for her mum and feels her mother's wishes should be respected 'if at all possible'. Jane, her second daughter, is adamant that her mother should go into a care home and to take any other course of action would leave her mother in serious risk and danger. The medical team are of the opinion that Mrs Terrell should probably be admitted to a care home. However, they have supported a discharge back to her home and have been persuaded by the improvement in Mrs Terrell's general health and well-being. The team now feel that medication and diet could be controlled and sustained in her home environment if the resources are there.

The role of care planning in intervention

It is generally accepted that the means of addressing need is confirmed via a care plan. Although the requirement to produce a care plan is not defined in legislative terms, the *NHSCCA* s47 states that 'having regard to the results of that assessment, shall then decide whether … needs call for the provision of them by any such service'. As a matter of good practice, any intervention should be underpinned by clarity about its objectives. Social workers should ask themselves the following questions:

● What are you trying to achieve?
● Why?
● How are you going to do it?
● What outcomes do you have in mind?

A clear set of objectives does not mean that interventions must be inflexible and unchangeable, far from it. A clear sense of purpose in an intervention provides a basis for monitoring and evaluation; if there is no plan at all, or the plan is vague and general, then it is very difficult to make any comment about whether an intervention or strategy is 'working' or not. Without goals of intervention, it is difficult to comment on whether part of the plan is more successful than others, and it is then difficult to assess why this might be the case and what action might be needed to resolve the difficulties. Apart from providing a basis for evaluation and monitoring, a care plan should confirm and provide the following:

● Agreement between a service user and practitioner about the needs that are being addressed and the way they will be addressed. This should be underpinned by a participative approach where service users are enabled to discuss or explore their preferences in terms of ways in which needs may be met or addressed. If a care plan includes input from other agencies and professionals, then their agreement should also include the care plan.

● An opportunity to identify specific preferences of service users and create a space for identifying need across a range of domains, not just focusing on physical need but also concerned with other aspects of life appropriate to the person's needs.

● A potential time frame for intervention although, of course, a significant number of care plans will address needs that are likely to be long term. Even in this situation though, it is important for care plans to indicate a date to review the care/support or interventions that are planned (see below).

● A timetable of care and support plans or care arrangements for a service user and other interested parties to be able to refer to. This may be particularly important when, for example, care arrangements are new and people may be struggling to recall the different elements of the arrangement. This might be particularly an issue for a person receiving a complex range of support and interventions.

● Information on the cost or contribution by the service user to their care.

● Important contact information, for example, for people responsible for providing services or interventions for the person and for the service user.

● An opportunity to identify and clarify the role of workers and the specifics of the intervention (for example, information on moving and handling techniques; information on mobilising a person).

● Opportunities to identify possible boundaries or limitations to input based on relevant issues regarding policy (for example, moving and handling, health and safety).

It is considered good practice for a care plan to be provided to confirm any service, no matter how 'simple' or straightforward (Brammer, 2003). Care plans must 'fit' the complexity of response to meeting need; for example, a very simple care plan might be provided, for example, for single items of equipment, such as a raised toilet seat and perching stool for a person recovering from a hip replacement operation. In contrast, the intervention and subsequent care plan for Mrs Terrell's discharge should reflect the complexity of her need and the arrangements put in place to address those needs.

A range of factors will shape the objectives of any intervention. Service user's views and perspectives, agency policy and provision and individual worker issues will inevitably interact and impact on the interventions and services ultimately provided. The development of an agreed course of action and intervention should ensure the participation of the service user and be underpinned by practice values which are explicit in promoting self-determination and countering discriminations (Hughes, 1995). The active involvement and participation of older people in planning responses to their own needs have not, until relatively recently, been a significant preoccupation in social and health care. Allen et al. (1992) argued from their research with older people receiving services, that choice was largely exercised by refusal or discontinuation of a service. Failure to explicitly address user participation and empowerment will result in the danger of achieving a mechanistic definition of a limited range of needs 'solved' by an equally limited range of off-the-peg service solutions. Minimally, involvement in planning interventions and care planning should focus on enabling older people to be as involved as they can or wish to be in identifying, agreeing and analysing their needs and how they should be addressed through intervention and care planning. This means, for example, actively listening to older person's accounts of aspects of their lives, which may influence both the experience of need and the ways that those needs may be most appropriately addressed. Mrs Terrell, for example, may identify the disruption to her spiritual life as a more significant issue than getting her clothes washed. It is, moreover, important that social workers encourage and enable discussions with older people about their preferences in the ways that those needs might be met. People's preferences may be influenced by long-standing continuities (for example, always eating a hot meal in the middle of the day) that they feel anxious or reluctant to change; we all have ways of doing things or personal preferences, which we try to ensure are met in our own lives and homes. Why should older people be an exception to this? Information about people's preferred lifestyle may give us clues about ways that needs may be more appropriately met. For example, someone who has been and continues to be very sociable may prefer needs to be met in a way which focuses on access to social contact (for example, a drop-in lunch facility or community church meeting rather than a solitary meal at home). It is essential to hear an older person's views about the changes they have experienced and the ways in which these impact on their lives. This may mean that long-standing continuities or preferences have to be amended or relinquished and new ways found to adapt to or come to terms with the change (Ray, 2000a). For example, a person with severe mobility difficulties who has always gone out a great deal in the past MAY choose to reduce this activity in order to preserve energy to continue with other important aspects of their day-to-day life. Attempting challenges may also be seen as a strength in people's lives.

Older people should have the opportunity to discuss the potential implications of interventions and care arrangements. For example, it is important for an older person who has not received home care before to be made aware of the fact that this arrangement will mean having visitors every day (or at the agreed frequency) and to some people, this may feel like an intrusion into their 'personal space' and revealing to others aspects of life that are traditionally kept away from public scrutiny (Aronson, 2002). Even if social workers and other agencies do all they can to try to ensure continuity, it is very unlikely that this will be entirely achieved. It may be important for older people to consider the implications of not always being able to have the same carer and to think about what, for them, would be acceptable and unacceptable levels of uncertainty. This means that workers have to go beyond a 'surface' discussion where the emphasis is placed on providing a helper, for example, to assist with having a bath. Rather, it might involve spending some time on exploring what the implications of this might be for the older person.

Older people should also know what the costs are likely to be of any support or interventions they receive. This may after all influence the sort of help that older people wish to make use of. A discussion about cost and what an older person can afford may also reveal that the person is not claiming their full entitlement to benefits. Helping a person to claim their entitlements may, in turn, comprise an important aspect of an intervention and go some way towards improving the financial disadvantage a person is experiencing. Finally, participation should also involve being honest or 'transparent' about what cannot be achieved. This can be a difficult process as it is never easy giving bad news. But service users do have the right to know, for example, if finding domiciliary care to arrive at 6 in the morning cannot be found. This may prevent service users feeling let down because their expectations were informed by accurate information.

Working in partnership with service users to identify need and potential responses to them is also overlaid by a requirement to engage with and work with other professionals involved and families. Interventions to plan for Mrs Terrell's safe discharge will inevitably be influenced by, for example, the fact that there are a number of people who did not share the same views about Mrs Terrell's discharge from hospital. The following issues are likely to be relevant when considering the system that surrounds Mrs Terrell:

● Different perspectives and opinions about the 'inevitability of dependency' in dementia; how does Mrs Terrell stay at the centre of the picture when, for example, some people may view a person with dementia as, almost inevitably, unable to give an opinion about their own life or lifestyle preferences?
● Diverse definitions and opinions about risk; what constitutes risk and whether risk taking is desirable and possible; and what degree of risk should be appropriately tolerated?
● Different views about the rights of individual service users to make decisions and choices about their lives; this is often made more complex by issues in deciding whether a person can make an informed decision.
● Who might be involved in providing support and care for Mrs Terrell and how will those roles, responsibilities and boundaries be negotiated?
● What might be possible and achievable in terms of creating solutions to Mrs Terrell's needs and can they be resourced and financed appropriately?

First of all, it is essential that interventions and associated care plans relate to the needs and circumstances identified in the person's assessment. This means, for example, an analysis of the needs that have emerged from assessment must be undertaken. Analysing a need in order to establish why it exists may evidence a complexity that might not have been initially anticipated. Consider this example, if Mrs Terrell were to go home.

One obvious 'service solution' to Mrs Terrell's weight loss and unstable diabetes would be to provide meals on wheels on a daily basis. However, an analysis of the need for meals suggests that meals on wheels may not meet need in an acceptable way. Consider first of all the contextual factors impacting on Mrs Terrell's well-being:

- Mrs Terrell appears to be depressed and this may act as a disincentive to eating, especially alone.
- Mrs Terrell's well-being may be adversely affected by loss and change; the death of her husband and closure of her church may contribute to a loss of identity. And of course, the loss of a lifelong partner is likely to result in the loss of a person to share a meal with and for women, in particular, a person to prepare a meal for.
- Mrs Terrell has lost important social, spiritual and emotional contacts with people with whom she can communicate in her language of heritage.
- Mrs Terrell may feel low and anxious as she has to live daily with the realities of having memory difficulties and the challenges and disruptions that accompany this.

The experience of Mrs Terrell's cognitive impairments may be impact on her diet in the following ways:

- Mrs Terrell's short-term memory is not working well and she may forget to eat meals on wheels after they have been delivered.
- There is a danger that Mrs Terrell will reheat meals that have gone cold.
- There is the possibility that Mrs Terrell will not always recall that she has meals on wheels ordered and may therefore refuse them when they are delivered.
- If Mrs Terrell is not always able to orientate herself in time, she may be wakeful during the night and sleep during the day, and therefore not be available to collect the meals or feel too tired to eat them.

If we then consider Mrs Terrell as a 'whole person', the issue of nutrition becomes potentially even more complex as can be seen in Figure 6.1.

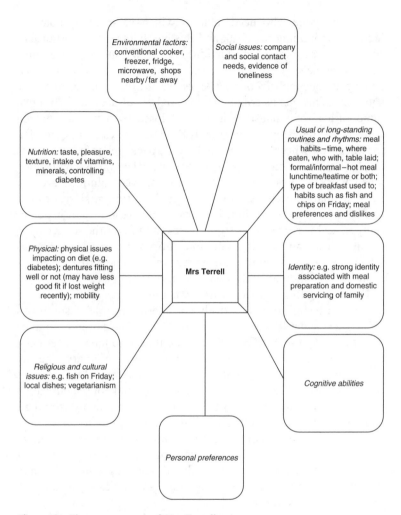

Figure 6.1 The assessment of Mrs Terrell

The provision of a meal therefore, is potentially about much more than simply receiving a hot meal each day. How, based on this deeper analysis of need might Mrs Terrell's needs be addressed while also recognising the organisational challenges that limit, for example, the provision of a home care assistant each day for the preparation of a meal 'from scratch'?

Not everyone who needs a meal will have so many complex factors surrounding the need, and this highlights the importance of considering people on an individual basis. We should not assume that everyone's needs are due to the same issues, are of equal complexity or simplicity or may be resolved by the same sets of service solutions. This means coming to the analysis of need with an open mind rather than one that has been closed by a message which conveys to the assessor that this is a referral/assessment/care plan for 'meals on wheels'; a 'domiciliary care package' or 'admission to care'. Clearly, maintaining an open, critical mind is challenging when work is pressurised and creative service solutions are not easily available. Perhaps, though, in the long run, analysis of need can be argued as important, if for no other reason, than it potentially saves the service user from distress and saves the service user, social worker and others time and effort when service solutions which are clearly inappropriate go wrong or are identified as unacceptable very soon after they have been put into place.

Developing this argument further, planning interventions should also mean being open to actively considering people's aspirations about their wider lifestyle. Analysis of Mrs Terrell's need for a meal might be linked to Mrs Terrell's potential need to have more social contact and also reconnect with her religious community. Sharing food in these contexts might be of more benefit to Mrs Terrell's overall quality of life and, indeed, may resolve many of the difficulties posed by delivering meals to the home. A limited analysis and an equally narrow response could fail to maximise quality of life and minimise risk; on the contrary, it may have little impact on quality of life and potentially create situations of risk – the very thing that the intervention was meant to address! Knowing your patch and having an awareness of its services and resources can contribute to creative solutions to need.

The single assessment framework includes the potential to undertake assessment of need on aspects of a person's life, including lifestyle, leisure, religious and cultural needs, and emotional issues. This breadth of assessment suggests, therefore, that a similar breadth should be applied to considering the identification of need and the subsequent development of interventions confirmed in care plans. Moreover, Hughes argues that we should 'be open to the possibility that older people have complex emotional or relationship problems which packages of practical services alone cannot address' (1995, p. 112). This represents a potential practice challenge in a work environment which may be increasingly likely to see older person's needs as being essentially physical and which can be adequately met by provision of services and aids. This narrow response may serve to reinforce stereotypes of older people as an inevitably dependent and homogeneous group where 'one size fits all'. It is also possible that the needs that workers do address will fail because other, more pressing or related needs are overlooked or ignored. There is a legislative duty (*National Assistance Act*, 1948, section 29[1]) for local authorities to 'provide a social work service and such advice and support as may be needed for people in their own homes or elsewhere'. In addition, the DoH Guidance (DoH/SSI, 1991 para. 47) states that 'the provision of advice and ongoing support for clients by social workers is very important in professional terms ... the language of care management can lead to this function being under-emphasised as compared to brokering for the provision of services by third parties'. This would appear to be the case and practitioners face the dilemma of identifying situations and circumstances in which direct work or additional one-to-one support is required, against a practice environment, which does not encourage it. But it is very difficult to work successfully or effectively with older service users where key needs are not recognised or a superficial analysis of need is utilised when a more complex approach is called for. Consider the following example.

Mr Smith was in crisis following the death of his wife. She had been his companion for over 50 years and more recently, provided him with important care as his arthritis had worsened. When a social worker visited him following an urgent referral, he was unable to engage in any discussion about his own needs. He was overwhelmed with grief and also guilt as he felt he should have 'known' that his wife was going to die and done something to save her life. The social worker, using a crisis intervention approach, identified some immediate help (meal preparation and a morning call) but also built into the care plan up to six meetings to help Mr Smith through the early days following his wife's death. This intervention proved importan in terms of helping Mr Smith cope, begin to work out what he could and could not do for himself and talk about his loss and help with practical arrangements. At the end of that time, Mr Smith had a support package in place and his social worker arranged to review the care after one month. Mr Smith had information about other services and resources that he might access and he knew he could contact his social worker if he needed to.

The importance of considering wider interventions beyond care brokerage is not an argument for directionless, open-ended and non-specific 'support'. Rather, it is an argument for being open to interventions that move beyond the provision of physical care services when those interventions are indicated by assessment. Any intervention should evaluate whether it has achieved what it set out to achieve and be informed whenever possible, by an appropriate evidence base (see Chapter 2).

Risk and care planning

Linked to the ability to analyse need is the importance of assessing an older person's strengths and skills, changes in their usual abilities and potential risks and dangers. Stevenson (2001) argues that risk must be analysed in conjunction with need for a number of key reasons. First, it reminds practitioners that risk may be caused or created by need and, moreover, that needs do not just happen at an individual level but also as a result of structural and institutional oppression and discrimination. For example, a person who is at risk of hypothermia in the winter may be at risk because of living in poor housing and poverty which may, in turn, affect their ability to pay for heating, upgrade and refurbish their homes and eat well because local shops have closed down and transport systems have deteriorated. Linking potential risk to need should also promote active thinking about how to creatively address risk in the context of preserving a person's skill while working with the fact that a person's abilities are declining. This means:

- weighing up risk against strengths
- balancing diverse opinions and perspectives
- negotiating possible resolutions
- openness in discussing observations, hypotheses, concerns and evidence
- the ability to weigh up potential solutions against the potential costs to the service user and/or their informal support network
- the ability to consider the value of potential resolutions against the resources required
- work within agency policy and advocate for the service user.

If we consider these issues in respect of Mrs Terrell, how might a care plan be co-ordinated and developed to address issues of risk against Mrs Terrell's rights to autonomy and to participate in decisions about her own life? Her social worker, in conjunction with the rest of the team, had to make use of her knowledge of Mrs Terrell, her understanding and knowledge base for positive dementia care, her understanding of risk assessment and risk taking as defined by the multi-agency risk policy that workers in her authority follow and her ability to negotiate with other agencies and Mrs Terrell's family. Throughout the whole process, she worked hard to make sure that Mrs Terrell had the chance to say what she wanted. Table 6.1 highlights how Mrs Terrell's social worker considered needs and potential risks against strengths and potential resources.

These ideas were discussed with Mrs Terrell and by the team as they worked on discharge planning. Discharge arrangements were put in place with a care plan which incorporated many of these ideas.

It is sound practice to ensure that copies of the care plan are provided to the service user, providing agencies and immediate carers (with appropriate agreement about sharing information). Failure to do so can mean that muddles and misunderstandings occur. A service user might for example, be trying to adapt to several visits a day from home care workers and visits from other agencies such as meals on wheels providers, transportation services and primary health care workers. Having a timetable to refer to can be very helpful. It is also important for people in the helping system to know what they should be doing in order to avoid important tasks or activities being overlooked or forgotten.

Moving into a care home requires that practitioners make an effort to record the wider needs of the person. As the home get to know the person, they will undoubtedly develop the care plan. But it is not acceptable to limit an initial care plan to a comment about the person requiring '24-hour care'. The unsatisfactory nature of this level of care planning becomes even more pressing when the person concerned has cognitive impairment and does not, perhaps, have family members, friends or supporters who can fill in the detail. As discussed in Chapter 2, the transition into a care home can be an emotional time with the loss of a home, neighbours and regular routines. Social workers need to be aware of the difficulties many older people will face in making this move and must not leave this emotional 'work' to relatives or care staff alone.

Table 6.1 Risks and resources

Need/Risk	Strength/Resources
Mrs Terrell is likely to be at risk from hypoglycaemic comas if she does not have access to a regular, balanced diet and medication.	Mrs Terrell has built up a relationship with home care who have called in a couple of times a week for the past two years to help with some shopping and have often helped out by giving Mrs Terrell some lunch. There is no reason therefore, why this visit could not be extended to include daily visits.
Mrs Terrell is often incontinent of urine during the day and also at night. This presents a significant need in terms of personal hygiene and laundry. It may present an associated risk in terms of skin care, infection and danger from slipping in urine.	Mrs Terrell has not been incontinent of urine during her stay in hospital. This is thought to be because she has an adequate intake of fluid each day and she is encouraged to go to the toilet for example, after coffee, meal times, before bedtime. This could be included as part of a home care visit/routine. Assistance with laundry may also be built into the overall support package.
	Kate has also hypothesised that Mrs Terrell was becoming disoriented partly because of her diabetes and also partly, because she could not orientate herself in the dark to the toilet. Kate has therefore, investigated the possibility of fitting a 'night time guidance': finding the toilet unit' which will fade up and fade down light when pressure sensors are activated by Mrs Terrell getting out of bed. Her way will be lit to the bathroom and back to the bedroom. A regular and balanced diet may well impact positively on Mrs Terrell's diabetes as will regular and appropriate dosage of medication.

(Continued)

Table 6.1 (Continued)

Mrs Terrell does not take her diabetes medication or her water tablets.	The local chemist is happy to put the medication into a 'dosette' box and home care staff are allowed to remind Mrs Terrell to take her medication. The chemist can deliver medication to Mrs Terrell at home or given the potential for Mrs Terrell to decline to accept it, the medication could be collected by the home care team as part of the domiciliary care plan. A regular visit from the diabetic specialist nurse could be arranged. This could provide important and regular monitoring of Mrs Terrell's diabetes. It is unknown how Mrs Terrell will cope with this as she does not know her. However, she is generally well disposed to nurses given her long career as an auxiliary nurse.
Mrs Terrell misses her church and religious life and this appears to be contributing her low mood and quality of life. There is also evidence that Mrs Terrell is most agitated during times when she would ordinarily have gone to church or been involved in church activities.	It is possible for Mrs Terrell to attend the women's group at Seatown once a week which includes a service in Gaelic. Many of the women in this group also speak Gaelic and are of Mrs Terrell's age and come from a broadly similar cultural background. This is rather untried, however, as Kate cannot establish how Mrs Terrell would cope with the change or the journey (some 20 minutes away in the car). Her daughter has said she may be able to help but is clearly very busy and has considerable child-care responsibilities. One possibility is to ask one of the congregation to collect Mrs Terrell in the car. Again, this is untried but may be worth attempting. Kate, as a short-term measure has arranged home services with the vicar who still has pastoral responsibility for the village.

(Continued)

142

Table 6.1 (Continued)

Need/Risk	Strength/Resources
Mrs Terrell has lashed out at her grandchildren during weekly visits to her daughter.	Kate has observed that Mrs Terrell can become agitated if there are too many people around or a lot of noise that Mrs Terrell has difficulty tracking and making sense of. It was felt that the home care would no longer visit the house on Sundays. Instead, home care would undertake hygienic cleaning as part of their involvement and this would allow Mrs Terrell's daughter to continue to visit but have a bit more time to sit with her mother. It may be possible to take one or two grandchildren to visit Mrs Terrell rather than her be faced with the whole family at one go.
Mrs Terrell has lost valued social roles as a result of the death of her husband and the closure of her church.	Kate has investigated the possibility of a volunteer visitor from the Alzheimer's Society sitting service. The idea is to work towards Mrs Terrell undertaking some sort of life story work with a focus on village life and the history of the village. It is feasible that the person provided could speak with Mrs Terrell in Gaelic.
Mrs Terrell is finding it very difficult to use the telephone.	Kate is investigating the possibility of using a picture telephone so that Mrs Terrell can call her daughter and other family simply by pressing a photograph of them. Kate has also talked about purchasing a large day and date clock which will also help Mrs Terrell to remain oriented in time.

Monitoring and review

Tibbs reminds us that a care plan is 'a living dynamic document that changes to meet the need of people involved' (2001, p. 77). The reality is that the hard work that goes into planning an intervention and developing a care plan may have to be undone and redone repeatedly and sometimes in quick succession. This may be particularly important to consider in respect of people with dementia but is true of other people with complex, changing or uncertain situations and circumstances. It is not always possible, for example, when planning a hospital discharge to be absolutely certain how a person will cope with an aspect of their daily lives or indeed, the proposed method of meeting a need. Moreover, a person's health may change and so a sudden deterioration may result in a need to urgently review, reassess and redefine the terms of the intervention. Sometimes, situations that are uncertain, changing or have risk attached to them can be very fraught and feel difficult to manage. It is not always possible to know with certainty how to manage a situation and asking for support via supervision, opinions of other colleagues and professionals and wherever feasible, discussing options with the older person and their families is a vitally important part of the decision-making process.

Reviewing care plans is an essential part of evaluating the outcomes or progress made on the basis of the interventions undertaken. A review also provides the opportunity of allowing participants to stand back and reconsider whether goals should be readjusted in the light of experience, evaluation and reflection. On this basis, Thompson argues that they are vitally important and we should not 'allow the pressures of work to stand in the way of reviewing and evaluating practice ... these are essential elements of good practice and so we need to use our time management and assertiveness skills to ensure that they are not "squeezed out" by other pressures' (2002, p. 222).

Mrs Terrell's care arrangements were reviewed by the community social worker. Jane had come from Canada to see her mother and was very upset that Mrs Terrell had been discharged from hospital. She had wanted her mother to be admitted to a nursing home and felt that part of her journey to Scotland might be to make sure that her mother was moved to a care home before she returned to Canada. The review went

(Continued)

(Continued)

well as it was evident that Mrs Terrell was generally doing well and her health was consistently better. The timing of the home care team visit in the morning was altered as they were coming a little too late; if Mrs Terrell had got out of bed and was ready for the day, it was very difficult to encourage her to participate in any hygiene routines and this impacted on her well-being. The home care team also felt that a longer visit twice a week would be beneficial as they were struggling to cope with the work they needed to do in the house to keep it organised.

The social worker and community nurse spent time with Mrs Terrell's daughter and they were able to explain the reasons why they were 'risk taking'. That to take some risk was beneficial to Mrs Terrell's quality of life and in achieving her desired outcomes (to stay at home). They were also working to achieve Mrs Terrell's desire to remain in her own home for as long as she could. Both members of staff acknowledged that they could not guarantee that Mrs Terrell's situation would not deteriorate to a point where admission to a care home would be the best option. Mrs Terrell's daughter was able to say something about her guilt at living in Canada and helplessness she felt at her mother's deteriorated condition. The nurse and social worker gave her their contact details and it was agreed that she would be kept informed of any changes and that she could contact either member of staff at any time to discuss her mother's progress.

Evaluating practice and interventions via a review process provides other important benefits. For example:

- opportunities to learn from feedback across professional groups thus developing practice;
- the possibilities of contributing to the evidence base by, for example, building an understanding of 'what works' in particular situations and contexts;
- opportunities to critically evaluate whether legal powers and duties were used appropriately; organisational procedures were followed; and actions were consistent with professional requirements and the principles of good practice were pursued (Thompson, 2002).

The following key questions form a sound basis for review:

● What were you trying to achieve?
● How were you trying to achieve it?
● How would you know when is it being achieved/was achieved? (Thompson, 2002).

The process of review builds on these three questions by posing further questions that can help us to retain a clear focus on what we are doing and why we are doing it:

● Were the original objectives appropriate?
● Are there obstacles to achieving the objectives?
● Were resources used to the best effect?
● Have the circumstances changed?
● Is the plan appropriate?

Addressing these questions in the context of a review should enable participants to assess the extent to which the original objectives were met or are being met and to reach a decision about the ongoing appropriateness of the objects and strategies used to meet them.

Older people should be encouraged and enabled to participate in review discussions as well as other key people such as other providers and informal carers and supporters. Older people themselves will be the experts on the degree to which their needs are being addressed and met, how the arrangements are working, and the extent to which arrangements may need to be adjusted. Consideration needs to be given to best ways to ensure the involvement of an older person in reviewing their care. It might be preferential, with the permission of the service user, to gather information from agreed people prior to the review and then inviting key people to the actual review. This might prevent the pressure associated with large, formal meetings. Such meetings might provoke anxiety and, indeed, feel very intrusive. People may sometimes appreciate having an advocate with them to support them in discussing aspects of their care. This may be particularly important when, for example, local authority criteria have changed and current care arrangements are being reassessed, particularly if care is being withdrawn (see, for example, Mandelstam and Schwehr, 1995). Of course, the nature and type of a review must match the complexity of the intervention.

As previously mentioned, care planning and monitoring are only one area of social work activity. Social work also has a rich repertoire of interventions which are aimed at helping people to change a situation that is painful or dangerous. In some cases, situations faced by older people cannot be changed, such as Alzheimer's disease, and so the intervention of social work may be focused on improving the quality of life for both older people and their carers. There are many direct interventions that social workers will use but here we select a few for discussion, which beginning social workers will experience in their practice.

Direct social work interventions

In Chapter 2 we outlined the importance of using theory as a framework for understanding and helping. In this chapter we expand on this in relation to interventions with older people, drawing on the case study material in previous chapters. We also outlined in chapter 2 various situations and transitions that people will go through and where a social worker may become involved if coping with the problem or transition becomes difficult. Inherent in the idea of transition is change and any social work intervention that accompanies transition needs to focus on enhancing the competencies with which a person brings to this change (Silverman, 1982).

Crisis intervention

When people are unable to draw on their coping skills during times of psychological distress, then crisis intervention may be appropriate. Studies have shown that this intervention has been successful in times of short-term crisis such as bereavement and loss (Rapoport, 1970) and traumatic events such as rape and domestic violence (Edlis, 1993). There are a number of ingredients in the experience of crisis, such as a precipitating event, a sense of loss, danger or humiliation, feelings of being out of control, events which may be unexpected; disruption to usual patterns and routines and uncertainty (Parry, 1990). One of the first studies to develop the theory behind this was Lindemann in his 1944 study of survivors of the Coconut Grove night-club fire in Boston. Reactions of sleep disorder, preoccupation with the image of the deceased, guilt, hostile reactions and a loss of patterns of conduct followed as reactions for many of the individuals who experienced grief. Those who sought help in their grief work found that they recovered in a shorter period than those who did not experience such help. Crisis intervention should therefore be time limited to the short term and should build on the coping capacities of individuals; it can draw on social work skills such as 'advocacy, bargaining, negotiation, use of empathy and appropriate challenging to achieve a constructive resolution of the crisis.' (Parker and Bradley, 2003, p. 105).

Task-centred work

Often crisis intervention is accompanied by task-centred work. A practical model for social workers is a task-centred approach, which focuses on the achievement of goals. It is a useful tool as small, achievable goals can be negotiated and this approach can be applied to individuals, groups and communities. Reid and Shyne (1969) and Reid and Epstein (1972) were the first to propose this method. The key ingredients of this approach are

- It is time limited: it has a beginning (setting the focus and goal) and ending (reviewing).
- It is task-oriented.
- It is Structured.
- It has clear aims and is specific.
- It concentrates on achievable goals.
- It systematic and appropriately flexible.
- It measurable.
- It focuses on removing blocks to achieving change rather than searching for the 'root cause' of the difficulties being experienced.

Accompanying a task-centred approach is often a contract or written agreement between the service user and the worker which identifies, specifies and prioritises the task in hand, together with the time period in which it is to be accomplished, and defines who takes action and how the review of the task will be achieved.

Mr Smith has been admitted to a residential home; he is severely disabled. He was previously a very active man in his community with many friends but no family support system. Because of the location of the home (the only place available at the time of his discharge from hospital), he is isolated from his network and has been referred to the social worker as, although not confused, is wandering outside the home.

(Continued)

(Continued)

The social worker identifies that Mr Smith's concern is to find suitable activity outside the home but the fears of the home owner are that he is 'at risk' from traffic on a busy main road. A task-centred approach is adopted with Mr Smith with the aim of integrating him into his new community; Mr Smith is asked to list his hobbies and explore any local voluntary groups that may help. Agreements are made about how and when he will do this. Although the social worker would be able to do this, giving Mr Smith the task motivates him to make contact with the relevant people himself and to arrange transport to the meetings in the local community. Specific tasks need to be identified and may involve the social worker doing other tasks e.g. getting together the list of church groups or introducing Mr Smith to a local vicar. As Mr Smith proceeds with the tasks, they may be modified to meet the changing situation. At each meeting a review should take place to agree changes. Flexibility is required in this approach so that extensions to the ending of involvement may also be made if necessary.

Task-centred work is often part of a larger form of intervention and can complement approaches such as Cognitive Behavioural Therapy described below.

Cognitive Behavioural Therapy

Different situations and events trigger different emotional responses or feelings and consequently cause different behaviour. Cognitive Behavioural Therapy (CBT) explores the relationship between these. The basic premise is that both cognitive and behavioural responses to events are based on our past experiences and what we think we ought to do in such situations and so is learned and can be changed. Change can come by relearning and adapting and substituting more effective responses. In older people it has been effective for treating depression and anxiety (Yost et al., 1987). CBT works best when older people do not have significant cognitive impairment, are communicative, actively agree to the intervention, are able to self-disclose to the social worker, have insight and are able to analyse their behaviour (McInnes-Dittrich, 2002). It is not appropriate for those people with serious memory problems or who lack concentration.

Yost et al. (1986) describe the process of CBT as involving four distinct phases.

1 *Preparation* where the social worker:
   (a) develops a relationship with the older person;
   (b) focuses with the older person on what needs to be changed;
   (c) discusses the symptoms, causes and functioning;
   (d) explains what CBT is and assesses whether they are suitable for this approach.

2 *Collaboration–identification.* In this phase the worker helps the older person to understand the connections between situations, events and feelings. For example, Mick was very anxious about having any help to resolve some of the difficulties with his housing. He was scared, following a failed 'clean-up' in which personal possessions were lost, that any more help would only make matters worse. As a result, the situation in the house was deteriorating rapidly.

3 *Change phase.* In this phase the social worker will work with the older person to recognise any cognitive disorder in their thinking. For example, Mick was convinced that everything had to stay the same in order to keep control of the situation, even though he appreciated that things had to change as his situation was deteriorating rapidly. The social worker used a number of techniques in the intervention, including written agreements, positive reinforcement strategies, and rehearsal and challenging Mick's distorted thinking.

4 *Consolidation and termination.* In this final phase changes are consolidated with a review of the older person's strengths and new skills they may have learnt as a result. Their self-awareness should then help them gain control in the future when other anxiety-provoking events arise (for a full discussion of cognitive-behavioural approaches, see, for example, Sheldon, 1995).

Counselling

The quality of the relationship between the social worker and the service user is fundamental to practice as we have argued throughout this book, particularly where counselling is concerned. Underpinning the relationship should be familiar principles of

● genuineness
● warmth

- unconditional positive regard
- empathy
- trust
- non-judgemental attitude
- non-directive approach.

Hughes (1995) notes that counselling may be difficult with older people who have difficult personalities or problematic behaviour, for social workers may not have unconditional positive regard or be able to empathise with them because of their lack of life experience. Challenging the attitudes and beliefs of older people may be difficult, e.g. challenging racist attitudes from a war veteran. Consequently social workers may fail to challenge, expecting older people to be entrenched in their ways! Such ageism has led to a lack of research on and use of counselling with older people. Thompson (1995) also believes that ageism can act as a barrier as the subjective experience of ageism and internalised oppression can lead older people to think they are not worthy of counselling.

Counselling can be applied in a number of settings with reference to bereavement loss and grief, traumatic past experiences, difficulties in relationships and painful transitions. Counselling skills, discussed in Chapter 3, may also be applied with a number of other approaches. A number of research studies have highlighted problems between generations of older parents and their children, many of which may have been left unresolved for many years (Phillips et al., 2003; Pillemar and Luscher, 2004). Role reversal may have taken place with the carer previously the cared-for child. Caring can be a difficult task and can lead to resentment, ambivalence and abuse within relationships if stress becomes paramount.

Different members of the family will have different viewpoints on the situation under review, what the stresses are, different expectations and different ways of resolving the issues (Scrutton, 1989). The main focus of counselling in this respect will be to get the family to 'negotiate new, mutually acceptable and agreed expectations, with each party being aware of what is expected of them and how much they can reasonably expect of others' (Scrutton, 1989, p. 92). This will involve encouraging family discussion, listening, identifying the tensions and interpreting them for the family in an impartial way.

Networking

One of the key skills which social workers need is that of networking with groups and communities on behalf of service users and social services organisations. Assessing networks both in relation to informal support systems and formal support systems from the user's perspective can be a useful assessment tool (Phillips et al., 2002).

Networking draws on the theoretical underpinning of community social work and radical social work as advocated in the 1980s in the UK. As McDonald (1999) argues, networking and radical social work drew on collective action and the links between the personal and the political. Advocacy and empowerment are also part of the links between political and personal levels. 'Advocacy generally involves people making a case for themselves and advancing their own interests, or representing others and supporting them to secure and exercise their rights on an individual or collective basis' (Dunning, 1998, p. 200). Whether social workers can act as advocates is a moot point as the prescribed roles that social workers hold through legislation and as agency gatekeepers can conflict with some definitions of advocacy, which stress the preferred wishes of the service user over the agency. However, social workers can use advocacy skills in their work, particularly where they are linked to user empowerment. Until recently the focus was on the user as 'consumer' in the notion of health and social care rather than the current shift to the focus on advocacy as citizenship. Advocacy stressing the citizenship rights of users can be empowering for older people in helping them to realise their full potential as well as rights and enhance intergenerational relations.

Life history work

Work with people with dementia has moved from a position of 'therapeutic nihilism' (Kitwood, 1997) to an area of practice that has undergone considerable development. Many of these interventions focus on maintaining and reinforcing the rights of a person with dementia to be included and feel positively engaged; to sustain emotional relationships and attachments, to feel secure and to be communicated with in a positive and appropriate manner. Life history work, for example, has been important in highlighting some key principles of person centred care; using a life history can help with planning support strategies, interventions and care planning.

Having information about a person's biography or life history can also greatly assist in making sense of aspects of a person's behaviour that might not be easily understandable. It is clear that workers who are aware of a person's life history can provide positive opportunities to validate and value a person with dementia as a unique individual. Developing a life history can provide a vital tool for good quality care for a person with dementia through their care journey. Life history work should go beyond facts about the person to include ideas about the person's attitudes, beliefs, values and traditions. Reminiscence is also a useful approach with people with dementia (Gibson, 2004).

Interventions with carers

In the past three decades services and support that can enable carers to continue in such roles have been developed. These include:

- information (about local services, financial support, nature of the illness or condition);
- skills training (handling, coping);
- emotional support (confidence building, expectations of role and valuing; someone to talk to; recognition of their own needs as individuals in their own right);
- regular respite and domiciliary support (home adaptations, continence service, help with transport);
- services which reflect differing racial, cultural and religious backgrounds.

What lessons are there for social workers in this area? *Caring about Carers: The National Strategy for Carers* (DOH, 1999) put forward a strategy for working with carers as citizens, with rights to expect a life of their own; maintenance of their health and well-being; confidence in the standard and reliability of services and the right to share caring responsibilities with service providers. It takes a three-pronged approach to such provision: information, which is accessible and relevant; support from a multi-agency perspective incorporating health housing and social care; and care (DOH, 1999).

What this also means for social work agencies is listening to carers; acknowledging their expertise in relationship working in partnership; looking at 'what works' and supporting attitudes towards carers within the organisation. The relationship between social care organisations and carers, however, has not always been one based on a concept of citizenship. Twigg and Atkin (1994) describe models of carers based on the relationship between carers and service providers with carers being seen by service providers as 'co-workers', 'resources', 'co-clients' or 'superseded carers'. The *NHS and Community Care Act* 1990 envisaged carers as 'resources' where they provided 'free' care to support the social care system, but with subsequent Acts stressing the citizenship principle, carers in theory should be seen as co-workers. However, there is evidence (Twigg and Atkin, 1994) that such a partnership is difficult to achieve in reality and often the notion of 'co-client' is stressed with the needs of the carer being stressed. The 'superseded carer' is where the relationship is encouraged to become one of independence and the carer gives up the caring role.

The relationship with carers highlights the differential power relationship between social workers and informal carers which has hampered any realistic advancement of a partnership between different agencies and carers in supporting them. Chambers and Phillips (2004) argue that this is due to several causes: the stereo-typing of carers as a unified group; paternalism by health and social care workers; resource constraints; the emphasis being on the burden of care; and the multiplicity of potential partners. Nolan advocates the 'Carer as Expert' model which should be used for the basis of assessment and intervention (Nolan et al., 1996). This model takes a lifecourse approach, focusing on the carer's experiences and is carer-centred, emphasising their strengths and coping skills.

One of the key objectives of the government's *National Strategy for Carers* (DOH, 1999) is to keep carers in employment for as long as possible and to enable re-entry to the workforce if they have spent a period of time in a caring role outside of the paid workforce. A number of initiatives have been introduced to enable this to happen (*Employment Relations Act*, 1999) giving carers in paid work the right to have time off to deal with a family emergency or the Work–Life Balance campaign to encourage employers to recognise the benefits to their organisation of flexible work arrangements.

Social workers will come across this issue not only in terms of working with carers as service users but also as employees of local councils. In a study of one local council social service, at least 10 per cent of the workforce was caring for older adults (Phillips et al.,

2002). Despite the agency providing social care, human resource staff had little knowledge of numbers and profiles of their staff in relation to their caring responsibilities; staff did not know of council policy to support them and much depended on individual line manager discretion. Child care was much more acknowledged than caring for an older or disabled adult. Many staff were also reluctant to share their situation with their line manager for fear of discrimination. It is important therefore to engage in greater sensitivity to carers' needs within organisations where social workers operate as managers and as workers. Being a professional in such situations can, however, be an advantage through access to knowledge.

The focus of this section is on carers but it must be acknowledged that for carers to be empowered, older people receiving care also need to be treated as full citizens. One of the ways in which this can be realised is by giving older people the right to choose their carer through direct payments. The *Carers and Disabled Children Act* (2000) presented possibilities for the extension of direct payments in supporting carers. Research finds that older people receiving direct payments felt happier, more motivated and had an improved quality of life than before (Clark et al., 2004). The corollary of such an improvement for carers could be considerable.

Conclusion

Care planning is a vital means of identifying and confirming the ways in which needs will be addressed. It provides a guide for those people involved in the care and support of a service user and importantly, a source of reference for the service user and their family and social network. Care plans should not merely focus on physical aspects of care but should also address wider areas of need, if appropriate to the intervention. Care plans provide an important source of evaluation; have the goals of the care plan been reached? Identifying clearly what the goals and tasks are and how they will be worked on, provides the basis for analysing why care plans are failing. The chapter has highlighted that care plans are not fixed in stone but are living and dynamic documents. Care plans will often change rapidly, especially, for example, when working with a service user with complex and changing needs. They also provide a vital source of reference and the potential for saying something about a service user's identity. Again, this is particularly important when working with people with cognitive impairment and/or those who do not have access to supporters and family members.

Finally, we turn to review the practitioner's role in light of our previous chapters. Acquiring knowledge and skills for social work does not stop on qualifying but continues as newly qualified social workers develop a professional persona and specialise in their role. In conclusion, we bring all the previous chapters together and outline what is needed to support and develop practice.

putting it into practice

Activity 1

What are the goals of a care plan? How can you make sure that older people are involved in developing their care plan?

Activity 2

How would you address the risks that Mrs Terrell faced in a care plan?

Activity 3

How would you ensure that older service users were involved in reviewing their care and support arrangements? (Consider this question from the perspective of people living in their own homes and people living in a care home.)

Further reading

Payne, M. (1997) *Modern Social Work Theory*. Macmillan, Basingstoke.

Phillips, J., Bernard, M. and Chittenden, M. (2002) *Juggling Work and Family Life*. Policy Press, Bristol.

Seden, J. (1999) *Counselling Skills in Social Work Practice*. Open University Press, Buckinghamshire.

Tibbs, M.A. (2001) *Social Work and Dementia: Good Practice and Care Management*. Jessica Kingsley, London.

7 | Conclusion: Supporting and developing practice

Introduction

This book has highlighted a number of the key practice issues, challenges and dilemmas that are commonly associated with social work with older people. How should we respond to each older person as a unique individual when we might feel that service solutions are 'off the peg' and devised on a one-size-fits-all approach? How should we manage the anxieties and uncertainties of risk and at the same time, seek to promote the active participation of an older person in making decisions and choices about their lives? How should we make sense of research to inform our practice? How can we keep up with the rapidly changing policy agenda and associated consequences for practice? These are just a few questions that are likely to be at the foreground of new and developing practitioner's assessment of their role. Access to comprehensive and appropriate support and development frameworks is crucial. However skilled, committed or tenacious a social worker is, s/he will also need support to maintain their commitment and tenacity and help, to develop and update their skills. Of course, practitioners as individuals have a responsibility for acknowledging that social work is a career-long process of learning and development. However, social workers also need to be able to rely on a predictable and good quality infrastructure of organisational support. This chapter discusses some of the key areas of support that a social worker may expect to draw upon for professional support and development. First, the role of induction is considered for new members of staff. The role and purpose of supervision are considered and the multiple functions of a supervisory relationship are explored. Finally, the role of ongoing professional development is discussed and the importance of keeping up to date and developing one's social work role is highlighted.

Professional development

Induction

As discussed in Chapter 2, social work with older people is located in increasingly diverse contexts; it is now common, for example, to work in multi-disciplinary teams and to have well-developed links with wide-ranging agencies and resources. Social work, like every other area of health and social care, has and continues to undergo enormous policy and practice change (refer to Chapters 1 and 2). It is even more important that social workers, whether they are newly qualified or very experienced practitioners, receive a full and proper induction when they move into a new service. The GSCC standards (Commission for Social Care Inspection (2004) National Minimum Standards Accessed, standard 3.1) highlight the importance of providing induction, training and development opportunities to 'help social care workers do their jobs effectively and to prepare for new and changing roles and responsibilities'.

An experienced practitioner will come to a new post with developed skills and abilities but even so, a change in geographical area, team or team function will still constitute a considerable learning curve. For example, changes may be experienced in the following areas:

- policy and procedures (for example, supervision, training, vulnerable adults, accessing resources);
- updating or learning new knowledge and skills in relation to the key tasks of the agency and the service user group it serves;
- the way services are planned and developed;
- what is available;
- local partnership arrangements and health and social care organisations;
- the availability of training and development opportunities;
- different approaches and degrees of user involvement in planning;
- different community profiles (e.g. demographic issues);
- team structures.

There is also the likelihood of social workers changing post to take on a job with greater responsibility, including supervising and managing other staff. Additionally, there are newly qualified social workers starting their first posts as qualified social workers. Whatever the circumstances, induction, when properly planned and given the necessary priority can be, as Peel has argued, be 'the first experience of training and development, when new employees have time to match the abilities they bring from their past experiences and learning to the requirements of the post' (2003, p. 311). Induction can be an important time for a social worker to begin to form a relationship with their manager and/or supervisor. This provides a good opportunity for the social worker and supervisor to plan in specific needs that a practitioner may have of induction and to think about short-, medium- and longer-term practice development goals.

The hospital social work team had a well-developed basic induction programme which included:

- meet the team (including understanding individual members' particular roles and responsibilities)
- aims and objectives of the team and its relationship to the overall provision of health and social care to older people in the community
- health and safety
- policies and key procedures.

Together with other opportunities, planned on the basis of individual need, such as:

- opportunities for shadowing and joint visits to allied teams and workers (for example, the hospital social work team)
- visits to other key agencies
- in-service training
- professional development plan.

When Kate arrived in the team from a different area, her main priority was to familiarise herself with other resources in the area. In discussion with her supervisor, Kate arranged to visit a range of resources as part of her induction. She achieved this partly by making arrangements to undertake her own visits of observation, and also went on some joint visits with other practitioners. She also attended three training days on single assessment procedures and Fair Access to Care arrangements and during these training days, met a number of key staff and representatives from a range of resources.

(Continued)

(Continued)

Kate and her supervisor worked out key goals for Kate to achieve as part of her induction. For example, Kate applied to attend the foundation course on the area Vulnerable Adults policy and identified a need to attend a course reviewing research developments in dementia care. Supervision sessions were arranged in the first three months to take place every three weeks as well as having opportunities for informal support and discussion from her supervisor and other team members. The proactive and planned support of staff members was identified in a joint review as a strength of the organisation and contributed to new staff members feeling valued and not simply another 'pair of hands'.

Peel (2003) argues that newly qualified workers often need special attention and support to ensure a smooth and satisfactory transition from new and newly qualified member to established member of staff. There is clearly a need to proactively assist in developing confidence, knowledge and skill through learning opportunities but also to achieve a balance between learning and the need to undertake work and be in practice. Supervisors are crucial in enabling newly qualified workers to achieve key goals in their first year of practice as qualified workers and to help work out the balance between practice and learning. Here is what the supervisor can do:

- encourage competent and accountable practice at an appropriate level;
- develop skill and confidence in managing the demands of a practice post (e.g. work load management, allocation, appropriate allocation in terms of complexity of work);
- underpin practice, skill and confidence via support provided in supervision, team meetings, joint work and in-service training;
- help the practitioner to become familiar with and confident about the aims and objectives of the organisation;
- enable the practitioner to understand and participate in developmental work;
- encourage and develop an appropriate standard of practice, which should be linked to the aims and objectives of the agency and informed by service user involvement and participation;
- encourage and develop critical reflection and a commitment to self-directed learning and development.

It is a mistake to think that induction is a luxury that can be ill afforded. It is certainly difficult to create spaces for learning, development and reflection to newly appointed workers and indeed, for longer-serving team members. But a failure to recognise the particular needs and requirements of new members of staff can in the end be costly. Workers may become disillusioned by the apparent lack of interest in or concern about their own development and well-being; practitioners may feel that they are working in isolation or are not supported in their practice, and workers may actually be struggling but feel, in a culture where induction is not prioritised, that they are discouraged from saying that they need help. This can contribute to a culture of defensive or poor practice which will undoubtedly impact directly on the experience of service users.

Supervision

Supervision has been described by Sawdon and Sawdon (2003) as a process which is both 'central and marginal' to social work; central because the most valuable resource of a social care agency are its workers; marginal, because despite the fact that supervision is at least in principle, accorded considerable importance, there is often confusion about what supervision should be for.

Chapter 2 discussed the increased orientation towards performance management and performance monitoring as part of new public sector management's commitment to demonstrated improved standards and accountability. Clearly, monitoring of work tasks, work load and output are important issues in supervision, but there is a danger that this agenda could dominate other important aspects of supervision, which it turn may have unanticipated consequences in practice and for service users.

Peter is supervised by the hospital social work Team Manager. As a manager, she is under considerable pressure to achieve the targets that have been set in reducing the waiting list for assessment. This is clearly an important goal as people were waiting an unacceptable time for assessment. The manager's approach has been to focus supervision on workload management, throughput of work and to ensure everyone is taking work from the allocation list. Peter feels that other aspects of supervision have been ignored. The last straw was when Peter was

(Continued)

(Continued)

told to 'close' the case he was working on against his own judgement. The service user in question had memory impairment and was no longer managing aspects of her personal care and hygiene or shopping and possibly paying her bills. Peter's assessment so far (supported by the existing evidence base about the time needed to form relationships with persons with memory and cognitive impairment) was that she needed time to build a relationship with a formal agency as she was suspicious that they were going to 'put her away'. Peter reluctantly closed the case but within a week, the lady had been referred back to the team as she was found by the police outside the Post Office at 3 a.m. The police had taken her to a residential facility overnight and the duty social worker visited her that morning to begin an assessment. The duty social worker did not know the lady at all; there was considerable irritation that the case had been closed, thus meaning that the lady had to go through the process of reallocation.

If Peter's supervisor had been able to offer a wider-ranging experience of supervision, it would be no guarantee that the lady in this case study would not have ended up in the same difficulty. But perhaps, a supervisor who was able to engage in dialogue with Peter would have more clearly understood Peter's rationale based on assessment, hypothesis and his own understanding of the evidence base on successful communication and engaging with a person with significant memory and other cognitive impairment.

Thompson (2002) in an analysis of the trends and debates to have taken place about supervision over the past several decades has identified the multiple tasks involved in a supervision relationship:

- monitoring work tasks and workload
- supporting staff through difficulties
- promoting staff development
- mediation (for example, between staff and more senior managers)
- ensuring that legal, organisational, policy and procedure are adhered to
- promoting team work and collaboration.

Lishman (1998) has highlighted a range of appropriate expectations in respect of the supervisory relationship. For example, supervision should be reliable and regular. Supervision is still sometimes not available or it can be cancelled with ease which communicates messages about the importance attached to supervision. This can clearly have an impact on the team culture, the well-being of team members and ultimately, the quality of services delivered to service users. Social work is complex and uncertain; practitioners are, for example, often engaged in the complex process of trying to balance the rights of older people to actively participate in decisions about their lives against the reality of declining health, abilities and finite resources. This can engender anxiety in practitioners, especially when they may be risk taking and working on complex arrangements to manage those risks. Given the level of uncertainty and associated demands, supervision reliably and skilfully provided is essential not only to the well-being of the practitioner, but also in terms of helping the practitioner to make decisions and engage in practices which will contribute positively to the lived experience of older people.

It is also important that supervision should take place in the context of mutual trust and with a clear awareness of issues of authority and responsibility (Lishman, 1998). In the same way that practitioners may engage in discussing with older people what their role is, what they may expect and how support and services may be delivered, supervision requires similar processes. Trusting relationships take time to develop and as discussed in the induction section of this chapter (see above), it is worthwhile spending some time exploring and confirming the nature of supervision, mutual expectations, and what will be delivered in context of supervision. Sawdon and Sawdon (2003) suggest that the process of engaging and setting a mutually beneficial working contract/agreement is very important in clarifying expectations and the role and purpose of supervision.

Supervision should also provide an opportunity to go 'below the surface' in analysis of problems and situations (Lishman, 1998). This should mean that supervisors provide opportunities to unpick and discuss complex situations. The work with Mrs Terrell provides a good illustration of the complexity of practice involved in working positively and in an empowering way with a person with declining cognitive powers. Most importantly, the supervision made use of the evidence base in relation to, for example, person-centred care planning in which individual biography forms a crucial feature of care planning and intervention (e.g. Killick and Allan, 2001). Knowledgeable and skilled supervision should draw upon research in order to ensure that practitioners are making active and best use of the evidence that exists. Social workers need opportunities to analyse their practice and to reflect on the outcomes of that practice. Moreover, social workers need to be able to feel that they have discussed potentially contentious practice; it is important to be sure, for example, that a proposed plan constitutes sound risk taking practice rather than leaving a vulnerable person in a situation of unacceptable risk. It is likely that a skilled supervisor, not intimately involved in a particular piece of work, can ask questions and make observations that will be helpful to a practitioner who is perhaps struggling to see their way through a mass of complexities and unknown factors.

Supervision should address issues workers experience as problematic (Trevithick, 2000). This may focus on the individual impact of aspects of the work. For example, a newly qualified practitioner may find attending formal meetings daunting and may benefit from support and help to overcome their fears. Problematic areas may also focus on practice issues, for example, a newly qualified worker may feel anxious about managing the complex procedures involved in helping a person move into a care home. It may be that the supervisor agrees an arrangement to shadow or co-work a case so that the practitioner can learn from a more experience worker and gain confidence in undertaking practice in a supported environment.

It is also important that supervision mirrors aspects of practice, for example, that it is conducted in an anti-oppressive manner (e.g. Lishman, 1998; Thompson, 2001). It would, for example, be unacceptable for a newly appointed black worker to be assumed to be the 'ethnic expert' in the team when other team members are not actively engaged in seeking to develop anti-racist practice.

It is essential in terms of the discussions relating to service users. In order to avoid the potential for dependency or a narrow focus of supervision, potential barriers to learning should be identified and explored as well as strengths and opportunities for learning. A social worker, for example, may feel resentful that the person who got the job they wanted is supervising them and their response might be to avoid all discussions about potential learning needs. Sometimes, practitioners feel worried about acknowledging difficulties if, for example, their previous supervisory experience was one where they were criticised and discouraged from identifying learning needs. Rather than seeing supervision as a positive and valuable opportunity to analyse, discuss and reflect on practice, the practitioner may view the experience as akin to being 'sent to the head master'.

Finally, from a team perspective, supervision with individual team members can feed into an overview of the learning and development needs across the team. This may help to decide how to allocate finite resources or might provide opportunities for creative and flexible approaches to team development. Practitioners with particular skills and abilities could, for example, provide a training input as part of a team meeting to update other team members. In her work with Mrs Terrell, Kate visited a SMART House and fed back to the whole team the ways in which technology was being used to create a supportive and enabling environment for people with dementia living at home.

The emotional demands and impact of social work

Older people, who receive social work services, will usually be facing personal challenge, change and uncertainty as a result of changing health or circumstances. They may be experiencing bereavement and loss, for example, the death of a long-term spouse or partner or the loss of a long-standing home. Of course, also, older people may be facing death. Additional complexities have been discussed throughout this book, for example:

● the feelings, views and wishes of family and others in the support network
● working with a number of agencies and resources
● changing practice contexts (legislation, policy, procedure)
● working to empower older people who are often facing deterioration in their abilities and associated possibilities of risk.

These complex and unique situations can take their toll on social workers – especially as they are multiplied by having a heavy case load, all of which will bring different challenges, issues and complexities. Of course, social workers are usually working in situations of organisational, policy and legislative change which also needs to be incorporated into the overall context of practice. It is important to know that supervision is a place where concerns or anxieties about the impact of practice can be shared, and the social worker may be able to feel reassured about those feelings and their practice.

Supervision is an important environment for social workers to be able to review their actions and check proposed plans.

> Kate used supervision to discuss her assessment and analysis of risk and risk taking in her work with Mrs Terrell. Kate was aware of her commitment to ensuring that older people had the opportunity to live where they chose. This was partly informed by experiences from her personal biography as she had resented her grandmother's admission to a care home before, in Kate's view, she needed to move. It was valuable to Kate, therefore, to be able to present her analysis of risk, the evidence that supported her assessment, and to discuss proposed plans. Discussions with her supervisor reassured Kate that she was proceeding appropriately and had not, for example, marginalised aspects of risk in her attempt to get Mrs Terrell back home. Kate and her supervisor were able to demonstrate appropriate decision-making processes, adherence to the local 'Vulnerable Adults' procedures and policy and theoretically informed interventions. Supervision in this context also evidenced accountability.

Clearly supervising and achieving a balance between managerial issues and wider issues of worker/professional development are a skilled process. But of course, social workers have responsibilities in terms of the way that they prepare for supervision. Social workers who approach supervision positively and aspire to it being a useful and integral part of their professional maintenance and development would, for example, do the following:

- be open to learning and development and also evidence sufficient self-awareness to understand how the work may impact on them from time to time;
- ensure that supervision is given an appropriate priority and that they receive it at the agreed frequency;
- be active in identifying their own learning and development needs.

Appraisal is another important aspect of supervision. Pattison has isolated three elements in typical appraisals; 'it is usually individual performance that is the subject of appraisal: appraisal requires assessment of past performance against previously agreed goals or targets. Goals and targets are set for future performance' (2003, p. 153).

Using evidence in practice

Chapter 2 introduced the importance of evidence-based practice in informing our practice with older people. The current gap between research and practice highlighted the fact that this is an area of enormous development and change. Individual practitioners have a stake in their active participation and engagement with the development of evidence-based practice through strategies identified in Chapter 2.

While it is crucial to acknowledge that authorities, resources and agencies have a key role in terms of supporting staff to become more aware of research and to make effective use of research, there is also the issue of individual practitioner responsibility. Achieving a social work qualification does not absolve the practitioner from the need to engage with ongoing effort to remain up to date in terms of developments in research and evidence-based practice, along with other aspects of the social work role. We have an ethical responsibility in terms of our duty to do the best we can and to provide the best we can to older service users who may be intensely vulnerable and definitely require skilled, knowledgeable and enabling practitioners. A failure to embrace knowledge as it evolves both at an individual and organisational level will stultify the organisation and impact on practice. Evidence-based practice may serve as an important challenge to those practitioners and managers who believe that services to older people should constitute little more than the provision of home care, meals on wheels and care home facilities.

The skilled practitioner has to make sense of and good use of evidence in complex practice environments. It is important to make sense of evidence in the context of practice wisdom and service user experience. Shemmings and Shemmings define practice wisdom as 'an accumulation of knowledge about what constitutes "best practice" through: observation and reflection on your own and other people's practice; talking to colleagues; reading articles in practice based journals; and hearing presentations from other practitioners in case discussions and workshops' (2003, p. 121). Evidence, then, needs to be considered in the context of an established and informed knowledge and skill base. But, of course, social work with older people does not stop there. Social work with older people operates in a climate of dilemma and change. Policy changes, the diverse needs of individual older people and practice and professional dilemmas abound. Social workers have to be equipped to respond to and engage with these complex worlds and at the same time, to aim to achieve good quality practice.

Conclusion: becoming a critical practitioner

The reality of practising in a dynamic and changeful welfare environment is evident. A crucial issue and a pertinent dilemma relate to the need to adapt to the changes and at the same time, to develop and also preserve the knowledge, skills and professional identity of social work. This is always important but especially so in the context of multi-agency work. Social workers should have a distinct set of skills, values and practice orientations that contribute to the multi-disciplinary context. As well as contributing their own knowledge and practice abilities, social work practitioners can also offer appropriate and important challenges to other practitioners. An integrated model of care, embracing psychological, physical and social aspects of the person is essential; if interventions are focused, for example, purely on physiological aspects of the person at the expense of other aspects, then social workers are well placed to challenge that orientation.

Knowledge does not stand still. The importance of evidence-based practice alone demands that practitioners make efforts to stay up to date with new developments. The relationship between personal commitment to lifelong learning and organisational support is highlighted in this chapter. Supervision, supportive appraisals and appropriate training and development can certainly contribute positively to a practitioner's professional development. The experience of being seriously listened to and offered the benefit of support, advice and challenge can also help to cope with the many stresses and strains evident in the world of social work.

To achieve constant growth and development as individuals it is important to have opportunities to learn, and the need for ongoing professional development has been highlighted by bodies such as the GSCC and employing agencies. Post-qualifying (PQ) awards are a common pathway to formal recognition of ongoing professional development and competence. The awards are achieved via accumulation of credits and there are different means of learning and study (for example, development of portfolio, credits achieved via academic courses, in-service training). It is possible, therefore, to design a post-qualifying award that recognises and develops competence in gerontological social work. Currently regional consortia consisting of partnerships between local agencies and educational organisations manage the PQ awards. Employing authorities or the GSCC website have useful information about awards and how to locate the appropriate regional consortium.

Epilogue

This book has covered some of the context of social work with older people as well as aspects of the job itself, including practice skills, assessment, care planning, monitoring and intervention. It has also addressed issues of support and supervision. Even a basic text such as this shows how complex the field has become. This is because we have a much greater understanding of the complexity and diversity of life experience and current circumstances. It is also because the context in which we work has become more complex.

One challenge is the need for practice to be more evidence based. There is more evidence now about what works and what does not and we need to be aware of this, and the fact that we increasingly need to justify our interventions in the light of research, like any other profession.

Much of the complexity of the task relates to the ageing of the population. Projections based on the 2001 census have been dramatically recast to suggest that there will be a lot more older people in the next 20 years than originally estimated because the current cohort of older people are living longer than expected. Another aspect of increasing longevity is in the ageing of groups of people who are living to retirement age for the first time; people with all sorts of disability such as learning disabilities. British society, perhaps most dramatically the pensions industry, has to face these increasing numbers. The long-term care sector has to change as housing with care is increasingly seen as a better replacement. How this will be financed is another major issue.

We are also in a whirlpool of government policies both about the lives of older people and about social work itself. Where is social work with older people to place itself? Is it to be closer to health organisationally? If it were, it would be to some extent a return to pre-1970 when older people were the responsibility of public health departments in local authorities. Over 30 years we have seen the pendulum swing, thus demonstrating that there are pros and cons of every organisational model; no one will be exactly right. We are also moving towards a workforce shortage, which will have profound implications for social work and social care.

It is ever more important that social work asserts its values in this context and ensures that its skills and knowledge are available. It is too easy to emphasise the very basic needs or health requirements and forget to give attention to the unique individual who has needs which may not be met by standard services. Needs assessment is one of the most challenging tasks if it is to be more than rationing.

Ambivalent attitudes to social work make it hard for social workers to feel valued themselves. They are not valued by the general public and have to deal with people who need help who are increasingly demanding and ready to complain. Emotions run high and often social workers are there to bear the brunt of them. In this context it is hard to have the extra energy to ensure that social work with older people continues to grow and develop. It should do so in part in relation to research findings, but also in terms of creative responses to meeting ever more complex needs in an ever more complex world. New groups of older people need attention. This book has drawn attention to older homeless people. Older prisoners and older people with complex and chronic disabilities are two groups with whom we need to engage (Phillips et al., 2000).

Finally, to return to the ethical issues with which social work will have to grapple. The obvious one is about resources and resource allocation which will be increasingly stretched by the ageing baby boomers. Euthanasia is an issue often linked to ageing whereas it is more appropriately linked to pain and quality of life. There are many issues concerning abuse, restraint and incarceration which need a lot more debate. Social work is in the thick of all of these and can make an important contribution.

This is an exciting and challenging field. It is also a field which is changing rapidly. Since the first edition of the book we have a better understanding of the varied needs and situations in which older people find themselves. We can no longer view 'older people' as a homogeneous group with simple needs; their lives and experiences add a complex and diverse dimension to the lifecourse. We are also able to respond to the needs of the minority of older people who need to draw on social work services, through legislative, policy and practice developments. As professionals we need to recognise our own ageing within this and reflect on our own experiences. In this way we hope this book has made a solid contribution to better informed and more confident social work.

References

Adams, R., Dominelli, L. and Payne, M. (1998) *Social Work: Themes, Issues and Critical Debates*. Palgrave, Basingstoke.

Age Concern (2000) *New survey of GPs confirms ageism in the NHS*, *ACE*, 17 May.

Age Concern (2002) *Age Concern and Mental Health Foundation Working Together: 4.12.02*. Accessed via www.ageconcern.org.uk 1 February, 2004.

Allan, K. (2001) *Communication and Consultation: Exploring Ways for Staff to Involve People with Dementia in Developing Services*. Policy Press, Bristol.

Allan, K. (2002) *Finding Your Way: Explorations in Communication*, Stirling: Dementia Services Development Centre.

Allen, C., Clapham, D., Franklin, B. and Parker, J. (1997) *The Right Home? Assessing Housing Needs in Community Care*. Centre for Housing Management and Development, Cardiff.

Allen, I., Peace, S. and Hogg, D. (eds) (1992) *Elderly People, Choice, Participation and Satisfaction*. PSI, London.

Alzheimer's Society (2003) www.alzheimers.org.uk/News_and_Campaigns/Policy_Watch/demography Accessed 1 March 2004 and 23 March 2004.

Appleton, N. (1999) 'Technophobe or technofan survey: findings of Technology for Living Survey'. Paper presented at Technology for Living Forum launch conference, 10 November, London.

Appleton, N. (2002) *Planning for the Majority: The Needs and Aspirations of Older People in General Housing*. YPS, York.

Arber, S., Davidson, K. and Ginn, J. (2003) *Gender and Ageing: Changing Roles and Relationships*. Open University Press, Buckingham.

Arber, S. and Ginn, J. (1991) *Gender and Later Life: A Sociological Analysis of Resources and Constraints*. Sage, London.

Arber, S. and Ginn, J. (1995) *Connecting Gender and Ageing*. Open University Press, Buckingham.

Aronson, J. (2002) 'Elderly people's accounts of home care rationing: missing voices in long-term care policy debates', *Ageing and Society*, 22, 399–418.

Atchley, R. (1989) 'A continuity theory of normal ageing', *The Gerontologist*, 29; 183–90.

Atkin, K. and Rollings, J. (1996) 'Looking after their own? Family caregiving among Asian and Afro-Caribbean communities', in W. Ahmed and K. Atkin (eds) *'Race' and Community Care*. Open University Press, Buckingham, pp. 73–86.

Audit Commission (1986) *Making a Reality of Community Care*. London, HMSO.

Baldock, C. (2000) 'Migrants and their parents: caregiving from a distance', *Journal of Family Issues*, 21, 2, 205–24.

Bamford, C. and Bruce, E. (2000) 'Defining the outcomes of community care: the perspectives of older people with dementia and their carers', *Ageing and Society*, 20, 5, 543–70.

Bauld, L., Chesterman J, and Judge, K. (2000) 'Measuring satisfaction with social care amongst older service users: issues from the literature', *Health and Social Care in the Community*, 8, 5, 316–24.

Becker, S., Aldridge, J. and Dearden, C. (1998) *Young Carers and their Families*. Blackwell Science, Oxford.

Bengtson, V., Burgess, E. and Parrott, T. (1997) 'Theory, explanation and a third generation of theoretical development in social gerontology', *Journal of Gerontology*: Series B: *Psychological and Social Sciences*, 52, 2, S72–S88.

Bennet, G., Kingston, P. and Penhale, B. (1997) *The Dimensions of Elder Abuse: Perspectives for Practitioners*. Macmillan, London.

Bernard, M., Bartlam, B., Biggs, S. and Sim, J. (2003) 'New Lifestyles in Old Age Health, Identity and Well-being in Berryhill Retirement Village'. Unpublished final report, Keele University, Keele.

Bernard, M., Itzin, C., Phillipson, C. and Skucka, J. (1995) 'Gendered work, gendered retirement', in S. Arber and J. Ginn (eds) *Connecting Gender and Ageing*. Open University Press, Buckingham.

Beth Johnson Foundation (2000) *Advocacy for People with a Progressed Dementia: A Case Study in a Hospital Closure Programme*, Staffordshire, Beth Johnson Foundation.

Biggs, S. (1997) 'Choosing not to be old: masks, bodies and identity management in later life', *Ageing and Society*, 18, 5, 553–70.

Black, J., Bow, R., Burnes, D., Critcher, C., Grant, G. and Stockford, D. (1983) *Social Work in Context: A Comparative Study of Three Social Services Teams*. Tavistock, London.

Blakemore, K. and Boneham, M. (1994) *Age, Race and Ethnicity*. Open University Press. Buckingham

Bond, J. and Coleman, P. (1993) 'Ageing into the twenty-first century', in J. Bond, P. Coleman and S. Peace (eds) *Ageing in Society: An Introduction to Social Gerontology*. Sage, London, pp. 276–90.

Bond, J., Coleman, P. and Peace, S. (eds) *Ageing in Society: An Introduction to Social Gerontology*. Sage, London.

Bowers, B. (1987) 'Intergenerational caregiving: adult caregivers and their ageing parents', *Advances in Nursing Science*, 9, 2, 20–31.

Brammer, A. (2003) *Social Work Law*. Pearson Education Limited, Harlow Essex.

Braye, S. and Preston-Shoot, M. (1995) *Empowering Practice in Social Care*. Open University Press, Buckingham.

Brearley, C.P. (1982) *Risk and Social Work*. Routledge and Kegan Paul, London.

Brechin, A. (2000) 'Introducing critical practice', in A. Brechin, H. Brown and M. Eby (eds) *Critical Practice in Health and Social Care*. Sage/ Open University Press, London, pp. 25–47.

Brown, H. (2000) 'Challenges from service users', in A. Brechin, H. Brown and M. Eby (eds) *Critical Practice in Health and Social Care*. Sage/ Open University Press, London, pp. 96–117.

Butler, I. and Drakeford, M. (2003) *Social Policy, Social Welfare and Scandal: How British Public Policy is Made*. Palgrave, Basingstoke.

Butt, J., Moriarty, J., Brockmann, M., Sin, C.H. and Fisher, M. (2003) *Quality of Life and Social Support among Older People from Different Ethnic Groups*. ESRC Research Findings: 23 from the Growing Older Programme. (http://www.shef.ac.uk/uni/projects/gop/index.htm

Bytheway, B. (1995) *Ageism*. Open University Press, Buckingham.

Bytheway, W. (1997) 'Talking about age: the theoretical basis of social gerontology', in A. Jamieson, S. Harper and C. Victor (eds) *Critical Approaches to Ageing and Later Life*. Open University Press, Buckingham, pp. 7–16.

Calasanti, T. (2003) 'Masculinities and care work in old age', in S. Arber, K. Davidson, and J. Ginn, (eds) *Gender and Ageing: Changing Roles and Relationships*. Open University Press, Buckingham, pp. 15–31.

Cameron, C. and Phillips, J. (2003) *Carework in Europe: UK Report*. www.ioe/tcru/carework/uk

Casey, M. and Holmes, C. (1995) 'The inner ache: an experiential perspective on loneliness', *Nursing Enquiry*, 2, 3, 172–9.

Chambers, P. (2000) 'Women's voices in bereavement', in M. Bernard, J. Phillips, L. Machin and V. Harding Davies (eds) *Women Ageing: Changing Identities and Challenging Myths*, Routledge, London, pp. 93–109.

Chambers, P. and Phillips, J. (2004) 'Working across the interface of formal and informal care of older people: partnerships between carers and service providers', in R. Carnwell and J. Buchanan (eds) *Effective Practice in Health and Social Care: Working Together*. Open University Press, Buckingham.

Charlesworth, J. (2003) 'Managing across professional and agency boundaries', in J. Seden and J. Reynolds (eds) *Managing Care in Practice*. Open University Press, Buckingham.

Chau, R. and Yu, S. (2000) 'Double attachment to double detachment', in A.M. Warnes, L. Warren, and M. Nolan (eds) *Care Services for Later Life: Transformations and Critiques*. Jessica Kingsley, London, pp. 259–72.

Clark, H., Gough, H. and MacFarlane, A. (2004) '*It Pays Dividends*': *Direct Payments and Older People*. The Policy Press, Bristol.

Commission for Social Care Inspection (2004) National Minimum Standards. Accessed via www.csi.org.uk/nationalminimumstandards

Connidis, I. (2001) *Family Ties and Ageing*. Sage, Thousand Oaks, CA.

Cornes, M. and Clough, R. (2001) 'The continuum of care: older people's experiences of intermediate care', *Education and Ageing*, 16, 2, 179–202.

Cosis-Brown, H. (1998) 'Counselling', in R. Adams, L. Dominelli, and M. Payne (eds) *Social Work: Themes, Issues and Critical Debates*. Macmillan, Basingstoke, pp. 138–48.

Coulshed, V. and Orme, J. (1998) *Social Work Practice: An Introduction*. 2nd edition. Macmillan/BASW, Basingstoke.

Counsel and Care (1993) *The Right to Take Risks*. Counsel and Care, London.

Courtenay, W. (2000) 'Behavioural factors associated with disease, injury and death among men: evidence and implications for prevention', *Journal of Men's Studies*, 9, 1, 81–142.

Cowger, C. and Snively, C. (1997) 'Assessing client strengths: individual, family and community empowerment', in D. Saleeby (ed.) *The Strengths Perspective in Social Work Practice*, 3rd edition. Allen and Bacon, Boston, pp. 106–22.

Cowgill, D. and Holmes, L. (1972) *Ageing and Modernization*. Appleton-Century-Crofts, New York.

Crompton, R. (ed.) (1999) *Restructuring Gender Relations and Employment: The Decline of the Male Breadwinner*. Oxford University Press, Oxford.

Cumming, E. and Henry, W (1961) *Growing Old: The Process of Disengagement*. Basic Books, New York.

Daatland, S. and Herlofson, K. (2003) 'Lost solidarity or changed solidarity: a comparative European view of normative family solidarity', *Ageing in Society* 23, 5, 537–61.

Dalley, G. (1996) *Ideologies of Caring*. Macmillan, Basingstoke.

Dalley, G. and Smith, R. (1997) *100 at 100: A Study of Centenarians*. Centre for Policy on Ageing, London.

Davidson K., Arber, S. and Ginn, J. (2000) 'Gendered meanings of care work within late life marital relationships', *Canadian Journal on Aging*, 19, 4, 536–53.

Davies, C. (1998) 'Caregiving, carework and professional care', in A. Brechin, J. Walmsley, J. Katz and S. Peace (eds) *Care Matters: Concepts, Practice and Research in Health and Social Care*. Sage, London, pp. 126–38.

Davies, M., Falkingham, J., Love, H., McCleod, T., McKay, A., Morton, O., Taylor, L. and Wallace, P. (1998) *Next Generation*. The Henley Centre. London.

Decalmer, P. and Glendenning, F. (eds) (1993) *The Mistreatment of Elderly People*, Sage, London.

Department of Health (1998) *Modernising Social Services: Promoting Independence, Improving Protection, Raising Standards*. Cm. 4169. Stationery Office, London.

Department of Health (1999) *Caring about Carers: The National Strategy for Carers*. Stationery Office, London.

Department of Health (2000) *No Secrets: Guidance on Developing and Implementing Multi-Agency Policies and Procedures to Protect Vulnerable Adults from Abuse*. Stationery Office, London.

Department of Health (2001a) *Medicines and the National Service Framework: Implementing Medicine-related Aspects of the National Service Framework for Older People*. DoH, London. Accessed via www.doh.gov.uk 1 February and 23 March 2004.

Department of Health (2001b) *National Service Framework for Older People*. Stationery Office, London.

Department of Health (2001c) *Valuing People: A New Strategy for Learning Disability in the 21st Century*. Stationery Office, London.

Department of Health (2001d) *The Single Assessment Process Consultation Papers and Process*, Stationery Office, London.

Department of Health (2002a) *Fair Access to Care Services: Guidance on Eligibility Criteria for Adult Social Care*. LAC (2002) 13. Stationery Office, London.

Department of Health (2002b) *Fair Access to Care: Implementation Questions and Answers*. Stationery Office, London. Accessed via www.doh.gov.uk/scg/facs 30 January 2004.

Department of Health (2002c) *Care Homes for Older People: National Minimum Standards*. Stationery Office, London. Accessed via www.doh.gov.uk/ncsc 25 January 2004.

Department of Health (2002d) *Guidance on the Single Assessment Process for Older People*. LAC (2002) 1. Stationery Office, London.

Department of Health (2003) *Improving Older People's Services: From Policy to Practice 2002*. Stationery Office. London. Accessed via www.doh.gov.uk/ssi/olderpeople03.htm

Department of Health and Social Security (1981) *Growing Older*. Cmnd. 8173. HMSO, London.

Department of Health/Social Services Inspectorate (1991) *Care Management and Assessment: Practitioners' Guide, Managers' Guide, Summary of Practice Guidance*. Stationery Office, London.

Dixon, S. (2003) 'Implications of population ageing for the labour market'. *Labour Market Trends*, February, 2003 Special Feature, Office of National Statistics. London, pp. 67–76.

Dominelli, L. (1998) 'Anti-oppressive practice in context', in R. Adams, L. Dominelli and M. Payne (eds) *Social Work: Themes, Issues and Critical Debates*. Macmillan, Basingstoke, pp. 3–22.

Dunning, A. (1998) 'Advocacy, empowerment and older people', in J. Phillips and M. Bernard (eds) *The Social Policy of Old Age*. Centre for Policy on Ageing, London, pp. 200–22.

Eastman, M. (1995) *User First: Implications for Management*. Chapman Hall, London, pp. 258–68.

Edlis, N. (1993) 'Rape crisis: development of a centre in an Israeli hospital', *Social Work in Health Care*, 18, 3–4, 169–78.

Estes, C. (1979) *The Ageing Enterprise*. Jossey-Bass, San Francisco, CA.

Eurostat (2002) www.europa.eu.int/comm/eurostat/

Evandrou, M. (1997) *Baby Boomers: Ageing in the 21st Century*. Age Concern, London.

Evandrou, M. (1998) 'Great expectations: social policy and the new millennium elders', in M. Bernard and J. Phillips (eds) *The Social Policy of Old Age*. Centre for Policy on Ageing, London.

Evandrou, M. and Glaser, K. (2003) 'Combining work and family life: the pension penalty of caring', *Ageing and Society*, 23, 5, 583–603.

Evers, H. (1993) 'The historical development of geriatric medicine as a speciality', in J. Johnson and R. Slater (eds) *Ageing and Later Life*. Open University Press, Buckingham, pp. 319–26.

Falkingham, J. (1998) 'Financial (in)security in later life', in M. Bernard and J. Phillips (eds) *The Social Policy of Old Age*. Centre for Policy on Ageing, London.

Featherstone, M. and Hepworth, M. (1989) 'Ageing and old age: reflections on the post-modern life course', in W. Bytheway (ed.) *Becoming and Being Old: Sociological Approaches to Later Life*. Sage, London.

Finch, J. (1995) 'Responsibilities, obligations and commitments', in I. Allen and E. Perkins (eds) *The Future of Family Care for Older People*. HMSO, London.

Finch, J. and Groves, D. (eds) (1983) *A Labour of Love: Women, Work and Caring*. Routledge and Kegan Paul, London.

Finlay, L. (2000a) 'The challenge of working in teams', in A. Brechin, H. Brown and M. Eby (eds) *Critical Practice in Health and Social Care*. Sage, London, pp. 164–86.

Finlay, L. (2000b) 'The challenge of professionalism', in A. Brechin, H. Brown and M. Eby (eds) *Critical Practice in Health and Social Care*. Sage, London, pp. 73–96.

Fisher, M. (1994) 'Man made care: community care and older male carers', *British Journal of Social Work*, 24, 659–68.

Fisk, M. (1996) 'Telecare equipment in the home: issues of intrusiveness and control', *Journal of Telemedicine and Telecare*, 3, supplement 1, 30–2.

Gearing, B. and Dant, T. (1990) 'Doing biographical research', in S. Peace (ed.) *Researching Social Gerontology: Concepts, Methods and Issues*. Sage, London, pp. 143–59.

George, L. (1982) 'Models of transitions in middle and later life', in F. Berardo (ed.) *Middle and Late Life Transitions*. The Annals of the American Academy of Political and Social Science. November. pp. 174–88.

Gibson, F. (2004) *The Past and the Present: Using Reminiscence in Health and Social Care*. Health Professions Press, Baltimore, MD.

Ginn, J. and Arber, S. (1995) 'Only connect: gender relations and ageing', in S. Arber and J. Ginn (eds) *Connecting Gender and Ageing: A Sociological Approach*, Open University Press, Buckingham, pp. 1–14.

Ginn, J., Street, D. and Arber, S. (eds) (2001) *Women, Work and Pensions*. Open University Press. Buckingham.

Gloucestershire Social Services (2003) 'Adults *at Risk: Procedural Guide for Professionals*. Gloucestershire Social Services, Adult Protection Unit.

Goldberg, E. and Connelly, N. (1982) *The Effectiveness of Social Care for the Elderly: An Overview of Recent and Current Evaluative Research*. Policy Studies Institute, London.

Gorman, H. (2000) 'Winning hearts and minds?' Emotional labour and learning for care management work', *Journal of Social Work Practice*, 14, 2, 149–58.

Grant, G. (2001) 'Older people with learning disabilities: health, community inclusion and family caregiving', in M. Nolan, S. Davies and G. Grant (eds) *Working with Older People and their Families: Key issues in Policy and Practice*. Open University Press, Buckingham. pp. 139–60.

Griffiths, R. (1988) *Community Care: Agenda for Action*. Stationery Office, London.

Grundy, E. (1999) 'Intergenerational perspectives on family and household change in mid- and later- life in England and Wales', in S. McRae (ed.) *Changing Britain: Families and Households in the 1990s*. Oxford University Press, Oxford, pp. 201–28.

Gubrium, J. (1993) 'Voice and context in a new gerontology', in T. Cole, P. Achenbaum, P. Jakobi and R. Kastenbaum (eds) *Voices and Visions of Aging: Toward a Critical Gerontology*. Springer, New York.

Gunnarsson, E. (2002) 'The vulnerable life course: poverty and social assistance among middle-aged and older women', *Ageing and Society*, 22, 6, 709–28.

Hall, R., Ogden, P. and Hill, C. (1999) 'Living alone: evidence from England and Wales and France for the last two decades', in S. McRae (ed.) *Changing Britain: Families and Households in the 1990s*. Oxford University Press. Oxford.

Hardiker, P. and Barker, M. (1999) 'Early steps in implementing the new community care: the role of social work practice', *Health and Social Care in the Community*, 7, 6, 417–26.

Hargie, O. (1997) 'Communication as skilled performance', in O. Hargie, (ed.) *The Handbook of Communication Skills*. 2nd edition. Routledge, London, pp. 7–28.

Harper, S. (1999) 'Social gerontology: a review of current research', paper presented to the Nuffield Foundation, Oxford.

Haton, C., Azmi, S., Caine, A. and Emerson, E. (1998) 'Informal carers of adolescents and adults with learning difficulties from South Asian communities: family circumstances, service support and carer stress', *British Journal of Social Work*, 28, 6, 821–37.

Havighurst, R. and Albrecht, R. (1953) *Older People*. Longman, London.

Help the Aged (2003) *Age Today: Housing, Homelessness and Older People*. Summer, Issue 4, Help the Aged, London. Accessed via www.helptheaged.org.uk 28 February and 22 March 2004.

Henwood, M. (1995) *Making a Difference? Implementation of the Community Care Reforms Two Years On*. Nuffield Institute/Kings Fund, London.

Heywood, F., Oldman, C. and Means, R. (2002) *Housing and Home in Later Life*. Open University Press, Buckingham.

Hochschild, A. (1979) 'Emotion work, feeling rules and social structure', *American Journal of Sociology*, 85, 3, 551–75.

Holstein, M.B. and Minkler, M. (2003) 'Self, society and the "New Gerontology"', *The Gerontologist* 43, 6, 787–96.

Hough, M. (1995) *Anxiety about Crime Survey: First Report*. Home Office Research Study No. 147. Home Office, London.

Howard, M. (2002) *Redressing the Balance: Inclusion Competitiveness and Choice: A Report on the Barriers and Bridges for Carers and Employment*. Produced for the ACE National Development Partnership.

Howse, K. (2003) *Growing Old in Prison: A Scoping Study on Older Prisoners*. Centre for Policy on Ageing and Prison Reform Trust, London.

Hudson, B. (2000) 'Inter-agency collaboration: a sceptical view', in A. Brechin, H. Brown and M. Eby (eds) *Critical Practice in Health and Social Care*, Sage/Open University Press, London, pp. 253–75.

Hudson, B., Hardy, B., Henwood, M. and Wistow, G. (2003) 'In pursuit of Inter-agency collaboration in the public sector: what is the contribution of theory and research?' in J. Reynolds, J. Henderson, J. Seden,

J. Charlesworth and A. Bullman (eds) *The Managing Care Reader*. Routledge, London, pp. 232–42.

Hughes, B. (1995) *Older People and Community Care: Critical Theory and Practice*. Open University Press, Buckingham.

Hunt, L., Marshall, M. and Rowlings, C. (eds) (1997) *Past Trauma in Late Life: European Perspectives on Therapeutic Work with Older People*. Jessica Kingsley, London.

Jack R. (1995) 'Empowerment and community care', in R. Jack (ed.) *Empowerment in Community Care*. Chapman and Hall, London, pp. 11–42.

Jackson, G. (1996) 'The use of neuroleptics in nursing homes', *Nursing Scotland*, 1,1, 22–3.

Jones, K. (1972) 'The 24 steps: an analysis of institutional admission procedures', *Sociology*, 6, 407.

Joseph, A. and Hallman, B. (1998) 'Caught in the triangle: the influence of home, work and elder location on work-family balance', *Canadian Journal on Aging*, 15, 393–413.

Joseph Rowntree Foundation (2000) *Planning for Older People at the Health/Housing Interface Findings*. April 2000. Accessed via www.jrf/org/uk/knowledge/findings/socialcare/470.asp

Kadushin A. (1990) *The Social Work Interview*. 3rd edition. Columbia University Press, New York.

Karn, V. (1977) *Retiring to the Seaside*. RKP, London.

Kelly, M. (2001) 'Lifetime homes', in S. Peace and C. Holland (eds) *Inclusive Housing in an Ageing Society*. The Policy Press, Bristol, pp. 55–76.

Kemshall, H. (2002) *Risk, Social Policy and Welfare*. Open University Press, Buckingham.

Kemshall, H. and Pritchard, J. (1996) *Good Practice in Risk Assessment and Risk Management*. Jessica Kingsley, London.

Killick, J. (1997) *You Are Words: Dementia Poems*. Hawker, London.

Killick, J. (1998) 'Learning a new language', *Alzheimer's Society Newsletter*, 4 July.

Killick, J. and Allan, K. (2001) *Communication and the Care of People with Dementia*. Open University Press, Buckingham.

King, R., Warnes, T. and Williams, A. (2000) *Sunset Lives*. Berg, Oxford.

Kings Fund (2002) *Briefing Note: Age Discrimination in Health and Social Care*. Accessed via www.kingsfund.org.uk 1 March 2004.

Kitwood, T. (1997) *Dementia Reconsidered: The Person Comes First*. Open University Press, Buckingham.

Laing and Buisson (2003) *Care of the Elderly. Market Survey, 2003*. London.

Le Grand, J. and Bartlett, H. (eds) (1993) *Quasi-Markets and Social Policy*. Macmillan, Basingstoke.

Lewis, J. and Meredith, B. (1988) *Daughters Who Care: Daughters Caring for Mothers at Home*. Routledge and Kegan Paul, London.

Lindemann, E. (1944) 'Symptomatology and management of acute grief', *American Journal of Psychiatry*, 101, 141–8.

Lishman, J. (1998) 'Personal and professional development', in R. Adams, L. Dominelli and M. Payne (eds) *Social Work: Themes, Issues and Critical Debates*, Palgrave. Basingstoke, pp. 89–102.

Littlechild, R. and Blakeney, J. (2001) 'Risk and older people', in *Good Practice in Risk Assessment and Risk Management*. Jessica Kingsley, London, pp. 68–79.

Lloyd, L. (2002) 'Caring relationships: looking beyond the welfare categories of "carers" and "service users",' in K. Stalker (ed.) *Reconceptualising Work with 'Carers'*. Jessica Kingsley, London.

Machin, L. (2001) 'Exploring a framework for understanding the range of response to loss: a study of clients receiving bereavement counselling', Unpublished PhD thesis, University of Keele, Keele.

Mandelstam, M. (1999) *Community Care Practice and the Law*. Jessica Kingsley, London.

Mandelstam M. with Schwehr, B (1995) *Community Care Practice and the Law*. Jessica Kingsley, London.

Mannell, R. and Dupuis, S. (1996) 'Life satisfaction', in J. Birren (ed.) *Encyclopaedia of Gerontology*. Academic Press, San Diego.

Manthorpe, J. (2004) *Championing Older People: Making a Difference: Findings from 209 Older People's Champions*. Better Government for Older People. BGOP Research Series No. 1, London.

Martin-Matthews, A. (1991) *Widowhood in Later Life*. Butterworth, Toronto.

Martin-Matthews, A. and Keefe, J. (1995) 'Work and care of elderly people: Canadian perspectives', in J. Phillips (ed.) *Working Carers: International Perspectives on Working and Caring for Older People*. Avebury, Aldershot, pp. 116–39.

Mayer, J. and Timms, N. (1970) *The Client Speaks*. RKP, London.

McDonald, A. (1999) *Understanding Community Care: A Guide for Social Workers*. Macmillan, Basingstoke.

McGrother, C., Hauck, A., Bhaumik, S., Thorp, C. and Taub, N. (1996) 'Community care for adults with learning disability and their carers: needs and outcomes from the Leicester register', *Journal of Intellectual Disability Research*, 40, 183–90.

McInnis-Dittrich, K. (2002) *Social Work with Elders: A Biopsychosocial Approach to Assessment and Intervention*. Allyn and Bacon, Boston.

Means, R. Morbey, H. and Smith R. (2002) *From Community Care to Market Care? The Development of Welfare Services for Older People*. Policy Press, Bristol.

Means, R., Richards, S. and Smith, R. (2003) *Community Care Policy and Practice*. 3rd edition. Palgrave Macmillan, Basingstoke.

Means, R. and Smith, R. (1985) *The Development of Welfare Services for Elderly People*. Croom Helm, London.

Means, R. and Smith, R. (1994) *Community Care Policy and Practice*. Macmillan, Basingstoke.

Means, R. and Smith, R. (1998) *From Poor Law to Community Care: The Development of Welfare Services for Elderly People, 1939–1971*. Policy Press, Bristol.

Mental Health Foundation (2003) *Adults in Later Life with Mental Health Problems*. London, Mental Health Foundation. Accessed via www.mentalhealth.org.uk 20 February 2004.

Metsch, L. (1996) 'Community and adaptation: ageing in place in retirement communities', *Dissertation Abstracts International: The Humanities and Social Sciences*, 56, 11, 4559–60.

Milner, J. and O'Byrne, P. (2002) *Assessment in Social Work*, 2nd edition. Palgrave, Basingstoke.

Moody, H. (1988) 'Toward a critical gerontology: the contributions of the humanities of theories of ageing', in J. Birren, V. Bengtson and D. Deutchman (eds) *Emergent Theories of Aging*. Springer, New York.

Morbey, H. with McClatchey T. and Means, R. (2001) *Housing Adaptations and Improvements for People with Dementia: Developing the Role of Improvement Agencies*. University of the West of England, Bristol.

National Audit Office (2002) *Tackling Pensioner Poverty: Encouraging Take-up of Entitlements*. Report HC 37, Session 2002–03: 20 November 2002. Stationery Office, London.

Nolan, M., Grant, G. and Keady, J. (1996) *Understanding Family Care*. Open University Press, Buckingham.

Nolan, M., Grant, G. and Keady, J. (1998) *Assessing the Needs of Family Carers: A Guide for Practitioners*. Pavilion, Brighton.

Nolan, M., Grant, G. and Nolan, J. (1995) 'Busy doing nothing: activity and interaction levels amongst differing populations of elderly patients'. *Journal of Advanced Nursing*, 22, 3, 528–38.

Nolan, M., Walker, G. and Nolan, J. (1996) 'Entry to care: positive choice or fait accompli? Developing a more proactive nursing response to the needs of older people and their carers', *Journal of Advanced Nursing*, 24, 2, 265–74.

Norman, A. (1985a) *Triple jeopardy: Growing Old in a Second Home-land*. Centre for Policy on Ageing, London.

Norman, A. (1985b) *Rights and Risk: A Discussion Document on Civil Liberty in Old Age*. Centre for Policy on Ageing, London.

OECD (2001) *Ageing and Transport: Mobility Needs and Safety Issues*. OECD, Paris.

Office of the Deputy Prime Minister (2001) *English Housing Conditions Survey (2001)*. Stationery Office, London. Accessed via www.odpm. gov.uk 20 February 2004.

Office of the Deputy Prime Minister (2003) *The English Housing Conditions Survey: Building the Picture*, HMSO, London.

Office of National Statistics (2001a) *General Household Survey: 2001*. Social Survey Division, ONS. Accessed via www.statistics.gov.uk 15 November 2003.

Office of National Statistics (2001b) *Living in Britain*, Social Survey Division, ONS. Accessed via www.statistics.gov.uk 15 November 2003.

Office of National Statistics (2003) Census 2001: Carers. www.statistics. gov.uk

OPCS (1995) *General Household Survey*. HMSO, London.

Øvretreit, J. (1997) 'How to describe interprofessional working', in J. Øvretreit, P. Mathias and T. Thompson (eds) *Interprofessional Working for Health and Social Care*. Macmillan, Basingstoke.

Parker, J. and Bradley, G. (2003) *Social Work Practice: Assessment, Planning, Intervention and Review*. Learning Matters, Exeter.

Parry, G. (1990) *Coping with Crisis*. Routledge, London.

Patterson, B. (1995) 'The process of social support: adjusting to life in a nursing home', *Journal of Advanced Nursing*, 21, 4, 682–9.

Pattison, S. (2003) 'Virtues and values', in J. Reynolds, J. Henderson, J. Seden, J. Charlesworth and A. Bullman (eds) *The Managing Care Reader*. Routledge, London, pp. 149–56.

Payne, M. (1997) *Modern Social Work Theory*. Macmillan, Basingstoke.

Payne, M. (2002) 'Coordination and teamwork', in R. Adams, L. Dominelli and M. Payne (eds) *Critical Practice in Social Work*. Palgrave, Basingstoke, pp. 252–61.

Peel, M. (2003) 'Managing professional development', in J. Seden and J. Reynolds (eds) *Managing Care in Practice*. Sage, London, pp. 303–28.

Perrin, T. and May, H. (2000) *Wellbeing in Dementia: An Occupational Approach for Therapists and Carers*. Harcourt, London.

Petersen, T. (2004) 'The developing world: a short window to address global ageing problems', Guest editorial, *Generations Review*, 14, 1, 2–4.

Phillips, J. (1992) *Private Residential Care: The Admission Process and Reactions of the Public Sector*. Avebury, Aldershot.

Phillips, J. (1996) 'The future of social work with older people in a changing world', in N. Parton (ed.) *Social Theory, Social Change and Social Work*. London, Routledge, pp. 135–52.

Phillips, J. (2003) 'Gerontology: Research Based or Policy Driven?' Presentation at Regional Making Research Count Launch, South West London, May.

Phillips, J. (2004) 'Crime and Older People: the Research Agenda', British Society of Criminology and Better Government for Older People Conference, March, London.

Phillips, J. (2005) 'Crime, ageing and society: the research agenda', in A. Wahidin (ed.) *Crime and Older People*. Willan, London.

Phillips, J. and Bernard, M. (2003) 'Caring at a Distance', Presentation at the British Society of Gerontology conference, Newcastle-upon-Tyne, September.

Phillips, J., Bernard, M. and Chittenden, M. (2002) *Juggling Work and Family Life*. Policy Press, Bristol.

Phillips, J., Bernard, M., Phillipson, C. and Ogg, J. (2002) 'Social support in later life: a study of three areas', *British Journal of Social Work*, 30, 6, 837–54.

Phillips, J., Ray, M. and Ogg, J. (2003) 'Ambivalence and conflict in ageing families: European perspectives', *Retraite et Société*, 38, 80–108. L'Europe du grand âge: entre familles et institutions, Caisse Nationale d'Assurance Vieillesse, Paris.

Phillips, J. and Waterson, J. (2002) 'Care management and social work: a case study of the role of social work in hospital discharge to residential or nursing home care', *European Journal of Social Work*, 5, 2, 171–86.

Phillips, J., Worrall, A. and Brammer, A. (2000) 'Older offenders in the criminal justice system in England', in M. Rothman and D. Burton (eds) *Elders, Crime and the Criminal Justice System: Myth, Perception and Reality in the 21st Century*. Springer, New York, pp. 253–73.

Phillipson, C. (1982) *Capitalism and the Construction of Old Age*. Macmillan, London.

Phillipson, C. (1993) 'The sociology of retirement', in J. Bond, P. Coleman and S. Peace (eds) *Ageing in Society*. Sage, London.

Phillipson, C. (2002a) *Transitions from Work to Retirement: Developing a New Social Contract*. Policy Press, Bristol.

Phillipson, C. (2002b) 'The frailty of old age', in M. Davies (ed.) *The Blackwell Companion to Social Work*. Blackwell, Oxford, pp. 58–63.

Phillipson, C., Ahmed, N. and Latimer, J. (2003) *Women in Transition: A Study of the Experiences of Bangladeshi Women Living in Tower Hamlets*. Policy Press, Bristol.

Phillipson, C., Bernard, M., Phillips, J. and Ogg, J. (2001) *The Family and Community Life of Older People: Social Networks and Social Support in Three Urban Areas*. Routledge, London.

Pillemar, K. and Luscher, K. (eds) (2004) *Intergenerational Ambivalences: New Perspectives on Parent-Child Relations in Later Life*. Elsevier, New York.

Postle, K. (2001) 'The social work side is disappearing. I guess it started with us being called Care Managers', *Practice*, 13, 1, 13–25.

Pritchard, J. (1997) 'Vulnerable people taking risks: older people and residential care', in H. Kemshall and J. Pritchard (eds) *Good Practice in Risk Assessment and Risk Management*. Jessica Kingsley, London, pp. 80–102.

Pugh, R. (2000) *Rural Social Work*. Russell House Publishing, Dorset.

Qureshi, H. (1998) *Living in Britain: Growing Old in Britain*. Centre for Policy on Ageing, London.

Qureshi, H. and Walker, A. (1989) *The Caring Relationship: Elderly People and their Families*. Macmillan, Basingstoke.

Rapoport, L. (1970) 'Crisis intervention as a mode of brief treatment', in R. Roberts and R. Nee (eds) *Theories of Social Casework*. University of Chicago Press, Chicago.

Ray, M. (2000a) 'Continuity and change: sustaining long-term marriage relationships in the context of emerging chronic illness and disability', unpublished doctoral thesis, Keele University, Keele.

Ray, M. (2000b) 'Older women, long-term marriage and care', in M. Bernard, J. Phillips, L. Machin and V. Harding Davies (eds) *Women Ageing: Changing Identities, Challenging Myths*. Routledge, London, pp. 148–67.

Ray, M. and Phillips, J. (2002) 'Older people', in R. Adams, L. Dominelli and M. Payne (eds) *Critical Practice in Social Work*. Palgrave, Basingstoke, pp. 199–209.

Reid, W. and Epstein, L. (1972) *Task-centred Casework*. Columbia University Press, New York.

Reid, W. and Shyne, A (1969) *Brief and Extended Casework*. Columbia University Press, New York.

Richards, S. (2000) 'Bridging the divide: elders and the assessment process', *British Journal of Social Work*, 30, 1, 37–49.

Rose, H. and Bruce, E. (1995) 'Mutual care but differential esteem: caring between older couples', in S. Arber and J. Ginn (eds) *Connecting Gender and Ageing: A Sociological Approach*. Open University Press, Buckingham, pp. 114–29.

Rowe, J. and Kahn, R. (1998) *Successful Aging*. Random House, New York.

Sale, A. and Leason, K. (2004) 'Is help easily at hand?' *Community Care*, 6–12 May, 28–31.

Saleeby, D. (1997) 'The strengths approach to practice', in D. Saleeby (ed.) *The Strengths Perspective in Social Work Practice*. 3rd edition. Allyn and Bacon, Boston, pp. 80–93.

Sawdon, C. and Sawdon, D. (2003) 'The supervision partnership: a whole greater than the sum of its parts', in J. Reynolds, J. Henderson, J. Seden, J. Charlesworth, and A. Bullman (eds) *The Managing Care Reader*. Routledge, London, pp. 306–14.

Scharf, T., Phillipson C., Smith A. and Kingston, P. (2002) *Growing Older in Socially Deprived Areas*. Help the Aged, London.

Schiller, N., Basch, L. and Blanc-Szanton, C. (eds) (1992) *Towards a Transnational Perspective on Migration: Race, Class, Ethnicity, and Nationalism Reconsidered*. New York Academy of Sciences, New York.

Scrutton, S. (1989) *Counselling Older People: A Creative Response to Ageing*. Edward Arnold, London.

Seden, J. (1999) *Counselling Skills in Social Work Practice*. Open University Press, Buckingham.

Sheldon, B. (1995) *Cognitive-Behavioural Therapy: Research, Practice and Philosophy*. Routledge, London.

Sheldon, B. and MacDonald, G. (1999) *Mind the Gap: Research and Practice in Social Care*. CEBSS/School for Policy Studies, University of Bristol, Bristol.

Shemmings, D. (2004) 'Adult attachment theory and later life filial relationships', unpublished PhD thesis. University of East Anglia, Norwich.

Shemmings, D. and Shemmings, Y. (2003) 'Supporting evidence-based practice and research-mindedness', in J. Seden and J. Reynolds (eds) *Managing Care in Practice*. Routledge/Open University, London, pp. 111–36.

Siddell, M. (1995) *Health in Old Age: Myth, Mystery and Management*. Open University Press, Buckingham.

Siddell, M., Katz, J. and Komaromy, C. (1998) 'Death and dying in residential and nursing homes for older people', Unpublished report to the Department of Health.

Silverman, E. and Della-Giustina, J.-A. (2001) 'Urban policy and the fear of crime', *Urban Studies*, 38, 5–6, 941–57.

Silverman, P. (1982) 'Transitions and models of intervention', in F. Berardo (ed.) *Middle and Late Life Transitions. The Annals of the American Academy of Political and Social Science*. November, pp. 174–88.

Skucha, J. and Bernard, M. (2000) '"Women's work" and the transition to retirement', in M. Bernard, J. Phillips, L. Machin and V. Harding Davies (eds) *Women Ageing: Changing Identities, Challenging Myths*. Routledge, London, pp. 23–39.

Smale, G., Tuson, G., Biehal, N. and Marsh, P. (1993) *Empowerment, Care Management and the Skilled Worker*. NISW, London.

Smale, G., Tuson, G. and Statham, D. (2000) *Social Work and Social Problems; Working Towards Social Inclusion and Social Change*. Palgrave, Basingstoke.

Stevenson, O. (1996) 'Changing practice: professionalism, consumerism and empowerment', in R. Bland (ed.) *Developing Services for Older People and Their Families, Research Highlights in Social Work 29*. Jessica Kingsley, London, pp. 204–14.

Stevenson, O. (2001) 'Old people at risk', in P. Parsloe (ed.) *Risk Assessment in Social Care and Social Work*. Jessica Kingsley, London, pp. 201–16.

Stewart, J., Harris, J. and Sapey, B. (1999) 'Disability and dependency: origins and failures of "special needs" housing for disabled people', *Disability and Society*, 14, 1, 5–20.

Sutherland Report (1999) *With Respect to Old Age: A Report by the Royal Commission on Long Term Care*. Stationery Office, London.

Tanner, D. (1998) 'The jeopardy of risk', *Practice*, 10, 1, 15–28.

Taylor, P. and Parrot, J. (1988) 'Elderly offenders'. *British Journal of Psychiatry*, 1532, 340–46.

Tesch-Roemer, C., Motel-Klingebiel, A. and von Kondratowitz, H.J. (2003) 'Quality of life', in A. Lowenstein and J. Ogg (eds) 'Old age and autonomy: the role of service systems and intergenerational family solidarity', unpublished Final Report. University of Haifa, Haifa.

Thomas, T. and Wall, G. (1993) 'Investigating older people who commit crime', *Elders, Journal of Care and Practice*, 2, 53–60.

Thompson, N. (1995) *Age and Dignity: Working with Older People*. Arena, Aldershot.

Thompson, N. (2001) *Anti-Discriminatory Practice*. 3rd edition. Palgrave, Basingstoke.

Thompson, N. (2002) *People Skills*, 2nd edition. Palgrave, Basingstoke.

Thompson, N. (2003) *Communication and Language: A Handbook of Theory and Practice*. Palgrave, Basingstoke.

Tibbs, M.A. (2001) *Social Work and Dementia: Good Practice and Care Management*. Jessica Kingsley, London.

Tinker, A., Wright, F. and Zeilig, H. (1995) *Difficult to Let Sheltered Housing*. HMSO, London.

Titterton, M. (2001) 'Training professionals in risk assessment and risk management: what does the research tell us?' in P. Parsloe (ed.) *Risk Assessment in Social Care and Social Work: Research Highlights in Social Work*, 36. Jessica Kingsley, London, pp. 217–48.

Tobin, S. (1996) 'A non-normative old age contrast: elderly parents caring for offspring with mental retardation', in V. Bengtson (ed.) *Adulthood and Ageing: Research on Continuities and Discontinuities*. Springer, New York.

Tomassini, C., Glaser, K. and Grundy, E. (2003) 'Demographic and other influences on trends in the living arrangements of older people', paper presented to the British Society for Population Studies and FAMSUP London, May.

Townsend, P. (1962) *The Last Refuge*. Routledge and Kegan Paul, London.

Trevithick, P. (2000) *Social Work Skills: A Practice Handbook*. Open University Press, Buckingham.

Twigg, J. and Atkin, K. (1994) *Carers Perceived: Policy and Practice in Informal Care*. Open University Press, Buckingham.

Twigg, J. (2000) *Bathing: The Body and Community Care*. Routledge, London.

UK Coalition on Older Homelessness website www.olderhomelessness. org.uk/ Accessed 28 February 2004.

Vincent, J. (2003) *Old Age*. Routledge, London.

Waine, B. and Henderson, J. (2003) 'Managers, managing and managerialism', in J. Henderson and D. Atkinson (eds) *Managing Care in Context*. Routledge/Open University, London, pp. 49–74.

Walker, C. and Walker, A. (1998) 'Uncertain futures: people with learning disabilities leaving institutional care: a case of double jeopardy?' *Ageing and Society*, 16, 125–50.

Walker, A., O'Brien, M., Traynor, J., Goddard, E. and Foster, K. (2003) *Living in Britain Results from the 2001 General Household Survey*. ONS, London.

Ward, D. and Mullender, A. (1991) 'Empowerment and oppression: an indissoluble pairing for contemporary social work', *Critical Social Policy*, 32, 1–29.

Warnes, A. and Crane, M. (2000) *Meeting Homeless People's Needs: Service Development and Practice for the Older Excluded*. Kings Fund, London.

Webb, S. and Levin, E. (2000) 'Locality and hospital-based social work'. in G. Bradley and J. Manthorpe (eds) *Working on the Fault Line*. Venture Press, Birmingham, pp. 45–70.

Weinberg, A., Williamson, J., Challis, D. and Hughes, J. (2003) 'What do care managers do? A study of working practice in older people's services', *British Journal of Social Work*, 33, 7, 901–21.

Wenger, C. (1984) *The Supportive Network*. George Allen and Unwin, London.

White, A. (2002) *Social Focus on Ethnic Minorities*. Office of National Statistics, London.

Yost, E., Beutler, L., Corbishley, M. and Allender, J. (1987) *Group Cognitive Therapy: A Treatment Approach for Depressed Older Adults*. Pergamon, New York.

Useful web pages

Action on Elder Abuse www.elderabuse.org.uk
Ageing and Society http://titles.cambridge.org/journals/journal
Better Government for Older People www.bgop.org.uk
British Association of Social Workers www.basw.ca.uk
Centre for Evidence Based Practice http://www.ex.ac.uk/cebss
Community Care journal www.communitycare.co.uk
Department of Work and Pensions www.dwp.gov.uk
DH www.dh.gov.uk
General Social Care Council www.gscc.org.uk
Joseph Rowntree Foundation www.jrf.org.uk
King's Fund www.kingsfund.org.uk
Making Research Count www.uea.ac.uk/menu/acad epts/swk/research/
mrc/welcome.htm
Office of the Deputy Prime Minister www.odpm.gov.uk
Social Care Institute of Excellence www.scie.org.uk
SSI 2004 www.doh.gov.uk/policy and guidance/health and social caretopics/
older people's services

Acts of Parliament

(1948) The National Assistance Act
(1983) The Mental Health Act
(1990a) The Children Act
(1990b) The National Health Service and Community Care Act
(1995a) Carers (Recognition and Services) Act
(1995b) Disability Discrimination Act
(1996) Community Care (Direct Payments) Act
(1998a) Data Protection Act
(1998b) Human Rights Act
(2000a) Carers and Disabled Children Act
(2000b) Race Relations (Amendment) Act

Index